REPRINTS OF ECONOMIC CLASSICS

THE

MATHEMATICAL

GROUNDWORK

OF

ECONOMICS

THE

MATHEMATICAL

GROUNDWORK

OF

ECONOMICS

AN INTRODUCTORY

TREATISE

BY

A. L. BOWLEY, Sc.D., F.B.A.

PROFESSOR OF STATISTICS
IN THE UNIVERSITY OF LONDON

REPRINTS OF ECONOMIC CLASSICS

Augustus M. Kelley, Bookseller
New York 1965

Original edition 1924.
Reprinted 1965 by arrangement with Mrs. Ruth Nicholson.

Library of Congress Catalogue Card Number
65 - 16995

PRINTED IN THE UNITED STATES OF AMERICA
by SENTRY PRESS, NEW YORK, N. Y. 10019

PREFACE

THERE seems to be no book in existence, at least in English, that presents in a coherent form the mathematical treatment of the theory of political economy which has been developed during the past eighty years or more. The more familiar parts of the theory are assumed by writers or indicated in footnotes or appendices, the less familiar must be sought in the treatises or journals in which they appear; the various writers on the mathematical theory have proceeded from different hypotheses and adopted different notations, and students are consequently hindered in the use of this very valuable aid to analysis. Though the simpler applications of mathematics made by competent writers and lecturers can be appreciated by any intelligent readers and students, the more complicated analyses are only within the power of those who have mathematical aptitude, and it is for them that this book is arranged. The actual number of mathematical theorems used is quite small, but among them are some uses of the calculus which do not form part of the usual elementary curriculum, and these are brought together in an appendix.

I have attempted to reduce to a uniform notation, and to present as a properly related whole, the main part of the mathematical methods used by Cournot, Jevons, Pareto, Edgeworth, Marshall, Pigou, and Johnson, so far as these are applied to the fundamental equations of exchange and to the elementary study of taxation. Since I cannot be sure that I have not in some cases misinterpreted these writers, I have not given many detailed references, and must content myself with this general acknowledgement of indebtedness. I have not intended to advance any new theorems in economics, nor do I claim any originality in mathematical results, for the few theorems which I have not consciously adapted from others may in fact already have been published. Perhaps, however, there is in my analysis a more definite attempt than has been usual to deal equally with the hypotheses of competition and of monopoly, to find a place for incomplete monopoly and to indicate how perfect competition and perfect monopoly are mathematically the extreme cases of a more general conception.

My thanks are due to Professor A. C. Pigou and Dr. H. Dalton for advice on the general contents of the study, and to Mr. L. R. Connor who has devoted much time to correction and verification of the detail.

A. L. B.

March, 1924.

CONTENTS

INTRODUCTION

ECONOMICS deals with the production, exchange, possession, consumption, and use of material goods and immaterial services. The whole subject of wealth and welfare has two aspects, one subjective, moral or psychological, the other objective or material. From the one we may consider the attainment by economic action of an abstract good, or hedonistically the pleasure or satisfaction derived from the possession or use of things, or the desire to obtain goods; none of which terms are arithmetically measurable. From the other we may have in view material goods and actual services which can be measured by quantity or by money value. At first sight it might appear that mathematical reasoning was confined to the objective aspect, but this is not the case. If we cannot measure, it is true that we cannot apply the arithmetical processes of addition and multiplication and their converse; but we may be able to detect equality and inequality, relationship, continuity, variation, and other properties which lead to algebraic expressions.

It is proposed in the following treatment to have in mind two entities; the one incommensurable, the satisfaction derived from economic goods or in some cases the desire to obtain them, the other measurable, e.g. the physical quantity of goods. The second may be compared with a measurable shadow cast by an undefined object. The more exact relationship is as follows: write $U(x, y \ldots)$ for an algebraic function of measurable quantities $x, y \ldots$; let it be so related to an entity we will call $S(x, y \ldots)$, where S is not a calculable function but the non-measurable satisfaction derived from quantities $x, y \ldots$, that the following postulates are satisfied.

Postulates. (1) When $x, y \ldots$ vary without affecting the value of $U(x, y \ldots)$, more x balancing less y, &c., $S(x, y \ldots)$ remains unchanged.

(2) When $x, y...$ vary so as to increase $U(x,y...)$, $S(x,y...)$ increases, and if U decreases, S decreases.

(3) When there are successive variations of $x, y...$, the first increasing U from U_1 to U_2, the second from U_2 to U_3, so that the second increase is greater than the first $(U_3 - U_2 > U_2 - U_1)$, then the second increase in S is greater than the first; the postulate still to be true, when less is written for greater.

The first and second of these postulates are fundamental. U is measured on a definite scale, like the height of a thermometer. To any point on this scale corresponds a level of satisfaction, to be compared with the personal sensation of heat. When U increases, when the thermometer rises, S the satisfaction is increased, the sensation of heat is intensified. But a movement of 5 points (5 degrees) on the scale does not give a corresponding measurement of increased satisfaction, the intensification of sensation is not measurable. The thermometer is calibrated; the imaginary vessel of sensation is not.

The first two postulates, together with the assumption that people in their economic actions aim at increasing their satisfaction, are sufficient to obtain all the equations of equilibrium and in general all propositions that depend on the direction as distinct from the curvature of lines or the concavity of surfaces. Propositions depending on the sign or magnitude of the second derived function of U, which can be identified in the sequel by a careful reader,* require the third postulate. In terms of our analogy we should have that if in two successive periods the thermometer rose 5 and 8 degrees, the intensification of sensation in the second period would be greater than in the first.

The first two postulates are sufficient to connect a maximum of S with a maximum of U.

For convenience of working it is assumed that $x, y...$ can move by infinitesimal steps, so that a value corresponds to every scale reading, and that $U(x,y...)$ is a continuous function, i.e. that to a small change in $x, y...$ corresponds a small change in U. The great part of the analysis, however, would hold with close approximation if the quantities moved by finite steps, if these were small. The difficulty, if it be one, could be met in part

* The third postulate is only required for pp. 13, 15, 55.

by the use of the calculus of Finite Differences, instead of the Differential Calculus, but the results would be akin, and the slight improvement would not compensate the increased complexity. We may leave this difficulty with the remark that in the rare cases where the things or services exchanged are not susceptible of continuous variation (in quantity or quality), the results from the equations require some adjustment.

Since some name must be given, U will be called the utility function. The utility to which it relates is that generally called utility or value in exchange.

I

SIMPLE EXCHANGE OF TWO COMMODITIES

§ 1. Marginal utility, indifference curves, offer curves.

Consider first the problem of two persons A and B interchanging two commodities X and Y. This analysis is used in the elementary discussion of barter, and by many writers in the fundamental treatment of foreign trade. The restriction to two commodities is equivalent merely to supposing that the possession of other goods does not affect the exchange between the two in question. The restriction to two persons is more important, since it rules out questions of competition.

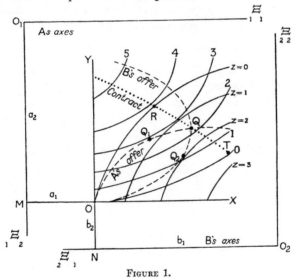

FIGURE 1.

A and B start with a_1 and b_1 of X and a_2 and b_2 of Y.

A receives x of X from B in return for y of Y.

After exchange A has

$$_1\xi_1 = a_1 + x \quad \text{and} \quad _1\xi_2 = a_2 - y,$$

and B has $\quad _2\xi_1 = b_1 - x \quad \text{and} \quad _2\xi_2 = b_2 + y.$

In the figure $_1\xi_1$ and $_1\xi_2$ are measured horizontally to the right and vertically downwards from O_1. $O_1 M = a_2$.

MOX is drawn horizontally to the right, and $MO = a_1$.

O represents A's initial position with reference to his axes $O_{11}\Xi_1$ and $O_{11}\Xi_2$.

OY is drawn vertically upwards from O, and YO produced to N, so that $ON = b_2$.

Through N a line is drawn horizontally to the right to O_2 so that $NO_2 = b_1$.

O_2N produced and $O_{22}\Xi_2$ vertically upwards form B's axes, viz. $O_{22}\Xi_1$ and $O_{22}\Xi_2$, and O represents B's initial position as well as A's.

The axes OX, OY are those on which x and y, the quantities exchanged, are measured.

Let $_1U(\xi_1, \xi_2)$ and $_2U(\xi_1, \xi_2)$ be functions expressing the utility to A and B respectively of the possession or consumption of ξ_1, ξ_2 units of the commodities X and Y.

Then $_1U(\xi_1, \xi_2) = {}_1U(a_1+x, a_2-y) = {}_1V(x, y)$,

and $_2U(\xi_1, \xi_2) = {}_2U(b_1-x, b_2+y) = {}_2V(x, y)$,

where the function V is defined by these equations, so that $_1V(x, y)$ measures the utility enjoyed by A after the exchange of y for x, and $_2V(x, y)$ measures the utility enjoyed by B after the exchange of x for y. For each value of y there will be an x which will just compensate A for the loss of y. The locus of such points is $_1V(x, y) = 0$, and this equation gives A's *indifference curve* through the origin, viz. OR.

For another locus of points, viz. $_1V(x, y) = 1$, A will gain one unit of utility, and so we have a family of curves $_1V(x, y) = z$,* in which the successive curves $_1V(x, y) = 0, 1, 2...$ are A's indifference curves. A movement from one point to another on the same curve does not change the amount of utility.

To any such curve, $V(x, y) = c$, a tangent at a point on it (x_1, y_1) is $(x-x_1) \cdot {}_1V_{x_1} + (y-y_1) \cdot {}_1V_{y_1} = 0$,†

where $_1V_x$, $_1V_y$ are the partial derived functions of $V(x, y)$, and

---

* This can be regarded as a surface, and in the subsequent argument the plane curves may be considered as contour lines of this surface.

† Appendix, p. 92.

$_1V_{x_1}$, $_1V_{y_1}$, are the results of writing $x = x_1$, $y = y_1$, in these derivatives.

This tangent passes through O if

$$-x_1 \cdot {}_1V_{x_1} - y_1 \cdot {}_1V_{y_1} = 0,$$

and therefore

$$x \cdot {}_1V_{x_1} + y \cdot {}_1V_{y_1} = 0$$

is the equation to the tangent from O to $V(x, y) = c$, if $(x_1 y_1)$ is on this curve.

For any named ratio of exchange $p = y/x$, the locus of exchange is $y = px$. This line cuts many of A's indifference curves and touches one, namely that for which $p = -{}_1V_{x_1}/{}_1V_{y_1}$, which it touches at (x_1, y_1).

It is evident from the figure that the curve touched is higher up the scale of utility than the curves cut. Consequently if A is free to choose the amounts to be exchanged at the named ratio, he will exchange y_1 for x_1.

As p varies, all the points of contact of the tangents satisfy the equation $x \cdot {}_1V_x + y \cdot {}_1V_y = 0$.

This is the locus of points (OQ_1Q) at which A is willing to deal, if he cannot control the price. It is called A's *offer curve*.

[In the figure

$$-x^2 - 2y^2 + 20x - 4y = 25z = 25 \cdot {}_1V(xy).$$

$$V_{1x} = \frac{1}{25}(-2x + 20); \quad {}_1V_y = \frac{1}{25}(-4y - 4).$$

The tangent whose point of contact to a curve is (x_1, y_1) is

$$(x - x_1)(-2x_1 + 20) + (y - y_1)(-4y_1 - 4) = 0.$$

This passes through the origin if

$$x_1(2x_1 - 20) + y_1(4y_1 + 4) = 0.^*$$

The locus of points of contact of tangents through the origin is therefore

$$x(2x - 20) + y(4y + 4) = 0,$$

i. e.

$$x^2 + 2y^2 - 10x + 2y = 0.$$

This is the equation of A's offer.]

---

* The equation to the tangent is then $x(x_1 - 10) + 2y(y_1 + 1) = 0$.

Similarly B's indifference curves are those concave to OY, OT is that through the origin, and B's *offer curve* is OQ_2Q, the equation of which is

$$x \cdot {}_2V_x + y \cdot {}_2V_y = 0.$$

§ 2. Equilibrium of exchange.

Assume in the first instance that the bargain is made as a whole, not the result of a series of exchanges.

B will try to take that point on A's offer curve which is most advantageous to him, which will be where A's offer touches one of B's indifference curves (Q_1). Similarly A will aim at a point Q_2, where B's offer touches one of A's indifference curves.

Let the offer curves intersect at Q. The double curve Q_1QQ_2 is called the *bargaining locus*. If B is the stronger bargainer he may secure a point between Q and Q_1; but if A and B are of equal bargaining strength, they will only both be willing to deal at the exchange rate and amount given by Q. In fact this is the position attained if the "formulae are regarded as representing the transactions of two individuals in, or subject to the law of, a market",* in which case there can only be one price, and where neither party is at an advantage with respect to the other. If this position is disturbed, it is to the interest of one or the other to revert to it.

In equilibrium we have, therefore, from the two offer curves and the identities given,

$$p = \frac{y}{x} = \frac{{}_1V_x}{-{}_1V_y} = \frac{-{}_2V_x}{{}_2V_y} = \frac{{}_1U_{\xi_1}}{{}_1U_{\xi_2}} = \frac{{}_2U_{\xi_1}}{{}_2U_{\xi_2}}.$$

These relations are obtained thus : †

$$D_{x\,1}\xi_1 = D_x(a_1 + x) = 1.$$

$${}_1V_x = D_{x\,1}V(x,y) = D_{x\,1}U(a_1 + x, a_2 - y) = D_{x\,1}U({}_1\xi_1, {}_1\xi_2)$$
$$= D_{\xi_1\,1}U({}_1\xi_1, {}_1\xi_2) \cdot D_{x\,1}\xi_1 = D_{\xi_1\,1}U({}_1\xi_1, {}_1\xi_2) = {}_1U_{\xi_1}.$$

Similarly $\qquad\qquad {}_2V_y = {}_2U_{\xi_2}.$

But $\qquad\qquad D_{y\,1}\xi_2 = D_y(a_2 - y) = -1,$

and $\qquad {}_1V_y = D_{\xi_2\,1}U({}_1\xi_1, {}_1\xi_2) \cdot D_{y\,1}\xi_2 = -{}_1U_{\xi_2}.$

Similarly $\qquad\qquad {}_2V_x = -{}_2U_{\xi_1}.$

* *Mathematical Psychics*, Edgeworth, p. 39.   † See Appendix, pp. 84-5.

These are the fundamental equations of equilibrium of exchange, and are due to Jevons.

At the position of equilibrium A's and B's indifference curves touch, and the common tangent passes through O.

$_1V_x = D_x V(x,y)$, y constant, is the *marginal utility* to A of an increment of X, when x and y are already possessed.*

Similarly $_1U_{\xi_1}, _1U_{\xi_2}$ are the marginal utilities to A of increments of X and Y when A possesses $_1\xi_1, _1\xi_2$, and $_2U_{\xi_1}, _2U_{\xi_2}$ are interpreted similarly for B.

§ 3. The contract curve.

If the exchange of y for x is not made as a single transaction from the position O (when A has a_1 and a_2, and B has b_1 and b_2) but from some other place, in other words if O varies: or, what comes to the same thing, if A and B do not know each other's position and make successive trial bargains † : then temporary equilibrium may be reached wherever a pair of indifference curves touch one another so long as each gains, or at least does not lose, utility.

At any such point

$$_1V_x/_1V_y = (-\text{gradient of } _1V) = (-\text{gradient of } _2V) = _2V_x/_2V_y.$$

The locus of such points, called the *contract curve*, is therefore

$$_1V_x \cdot _2V_y - _2V_x \cdot _1V_y = 0 \quad \text{or} \quad _1U_{\xi_1} \cdot _2U_{\xi_2} - _2U_{\xi_1} \cdot _1U_{\xi_1} = 0.$$

The intersection of the offer curves evidently lies on the contract curve. RQT is the contract curve in the figure. The segment RT between A's and B's zero indifference curves is that within which the bargaining can terminate.

§ 4. The demand and supply curves.

If y is eliminated from the equation

$$p = y/x = _1V_x/-_1V_y,$$

we obtain an equation between p and x, say

$$p = f(x).$$

* More correctly $_1V_x \cdot \delta x$ is an increment in utility due to an increase from x to $x + \delta x$.
† *Principles of Economics*, Marshall. App. F., p. 791. Edition 1907.

If Y is taken as being money, then p is the price of a unit of X, and the equation is that of A's *demand curve*.

Next eliminate y from the equation

$$p = y/x = -{}_2V_x/{}_2V_y;$$

the resulting equation, say $p = \phi(x)$, is B's *supply curve*.

[In the figure A's demand curve is obtained by writing $y = px$ in the offer equation. The result is

$$2p^2x + 2p + x - 10 = 0,$$

which may be written

$$p = \{-1 \pm \sqrt{(1 + 20x - 2x^2)}\} / 2x = f(x).$$

B's indifference lines are drawn from the equation

$$-x^2 - 3y^2 - 4x + 36y = 20z = 20 \cdot {}_2V(x, y).$$

$${}_2V_x = \frac{1}{20}(-2x - 4); \quad {}_2V_y = \frac{1}{20}(-6y + 36).$$

B's offer is $x(-2x - 4) + y(-6y + 36) = 0,$

i. e. $x^2 + 3y^2 + 2x - 18y = 0.$

B's supply equation is

$$3p^2x - 18p + x + 2 = 0,$$

or $p = \{9 \pm \sqrt{(81 - 6x - 3x^2)}\} / 3x = \phi(x).$

The contract curve is

$$(-2x + 20)(-6y + 36) - (-2x - 4)(-4y - 4) = 0,$$

i. e. $xy - 20x - 34y + 176 = 0.$

The offer, contract, supply, and demand equations are satisfied by $x_1 = 4.29$, $y_1 = 3.03$, $p = 0.707$.]

Both A and B gain by the exchange, A's gain being ${}_1V(x_1y_1)$, B's ${}_2V(x_1y_1)$.

[In the example ${}_1V(x_1y_1) = 1.5$; ${}_2V(x_1y_1) = 2.3$.]

§ 5. Elasticity of Demand.

The demand curve being $p = f(x)$, the quantity

$$\eta = -p/(x D_x p)$$

is called the *elasticity of demand*. $D_x p$ is generally negative (see

p. 55 below), the quantity demanded decreasing when the price increases, and η is then positive.

$$\eta \gtreqless 1, \text{ according as } p \gtreqless -x D_x p.$$

$$,, \quad ,, \quad D_x(px) \gtreqless 0.$$

$$,, \quad ,, \quad D_x(y) \gtreqless 0.$$

DEMAND CURVE.

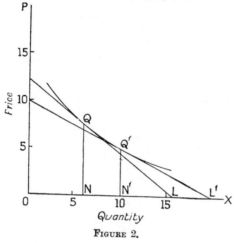

FIGURE 2.

In figure 2 $D_x p = -NQ/NL$, where $x = ON$ and $p = NQ$, and the tangent at Q meets OX at L.

$$\therefore \eta = NL/ON.$$

Figure 3 shows the values of $y = px$, where $x = ON$ $y = NR$, and represents the offer curve.

η may also be written $\dfrac{\delta x}{x} \div \dfrac{-\delta p}{p}$, where δx and δp are small finite changes (vanishing in the limit), and in this form is seen to be the ratio of a small relative increase in x to the corresponding small relative decrease in p.

When $\eta = 1$, $ON' = N'L'$, and by a well-known geometric property $L'Q'$, and therefore the demand curve, touches at Q' a rectangular hyperbola in which px is constant. It is also evident, since here $D_x(px) = 0$, that px is a maximum and is momentarily constant. At the same time $D_x y = 0$ and at the corresponding point of the offer curve (R') the tangent is horizontal.

As η diminishes and approaches O, $D_x p$ becomes very great negatively, and a great increase of price diminishes x very little ; ultimately when $\eta = 0$ the demand is said to be *perfectly inelastic*, and the demand curve is vertical.

On the other hand as η increases above unity, $D_x p$ becomes small, and a small change in p makes a great change in x. *Perfect elasticity* is reached when η is infinite and the demand curve horizontal.

OFFER CURVE.

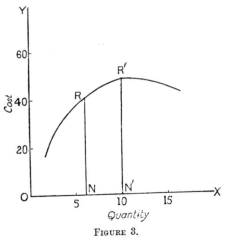

FIGURE 3.

§ 6. Money prices.

Let Y be money which A is paying and B receiving. Then $-_1V_y = {}_1U_{\xi_2} = \kappa_1$, say, is the marginal utility of money to A, and $_2U_{\xi_2} = {}_2V_y = \kappa_2$ its marginal utility to B.

We get certain simplifications if we suppose the marginal utilities of money to be unaffected by the sale and purchase of x, or, in other words, that A and B have so much money that this particular deal does not sensibly affect its marginal utility.

In this case A's indifference curves are parallel to one another ; for the gradient at the point (x, y) of the curve $_1V(xy) = $ const. is given by $D_x y = -_1V_x/_1V_y = {}_1V_x/\kappa_1$, and this depends on x alone since V_x cannot under the hypothesis be affected by y ; so that for any assigned value of x the tangents to A's indifference curves are parallel, and similarly for B's indifference curves.

The equation of the contract curve becomes

$$\kappa_2 \cdot {}_1V_x + \kappa_1 \cdot {}_2V_x = 0,$$

which only involves x and represents therefore a line (or conceivably lines) parallel to OY.

The offer curves are

$$x \cdot {}_1V_x - y\kappa_1 = 0 \quad \text{and} \quad x \cdot {}_2V_x + y\kappa_2 = 0.$$

A's demand curve is

$$p = \frac{1}{\kappa_1} \cdot {}_1V_x = f(x),$$

and B's supply curve is

$$p = -\frac{1}{\kappa_2} \cdot {}_2V_x = \phi(x),$$

without any elimination.

$$\left[{}_2V_x = -{}_2U_{\xi_1} \text{ and is negative.} \right]$$

In A's demand curve $\kappa_1 \cdot D_x p = {}_1V_{xx}$, where ${}_1V_{xx}$ is written for the second partial derivative of ${}_1V$ with respect to x.*

$$\therefore \eta = \frac{-p\kappa_1}{x \cdot {}_1V_{xx}} = \frac{{}_1V_x}{-x \cdot {}_1V_{xx}},$$

and $\qquad \eta \gtreqless 1$ according as ${}_1V_x \gtreqless -x \cdot {}_1V_{xx}$.

At this point we use our third postulate for the first time. It is evident that ${}_1V_x = {}_1U_1$ is positive so long as U increases with satisfaction, and greater satisfaction is obtained by increased possession of x. There may of course be a position of satiety when ${}_1V_x = 0$ and $p = 0$, and even of negative satisfaction when ${}_1V_x$ is negative and A would pay to have less of x. Similarly κ_1, κ_2, and ${}_2U_1$ are positive and ${}_2V_x$, ${}_1V_y$ are negative.

Now assume, as in fact is generally the case, that successive equal increments of x add less and less satisfaction, and, in agreement with this,

$$_1V(x+2\delta x, y) - {}_1V(x+\delta x, y) < {}_1V(x+\delta x, y) - {}_1V(x, y)$$

for all values of x and y in the problem.

* See Appendix, p. 90.

Then for a constant y successive steps of $_1V$ are of diminishing height, D_xV (i.e. V_x) diminishes as x increases and V_{xx} is negative.

In the figure (p. 5) the converse of this is seen, viz. that equal increments of $_1V$ need successively increasing increments of x, for the segments made by A's indifference curves on any horizontal line increase to the right.

Since κ_1 is positive and $_1V_{xx}$ is negative, D_xp is negative if the marginal utility of money is constant, and the demand curve falls continually to the right, and η is therefore positive.

If A and B are bargaining in similar conditions, it follows that $_2U_{\xi_2\xi_2} = {_2V_{yy}}$ is negative, and the segments of lines parallel to OY cut by B's indifference curves increase successively vertically. But if B is a producer employing labour and using materials, his position is no longer similar, and the argument no longer applies ; this condition is dealt with in detail later on (pp. 28 seq.).

§ 7. The utility surface.

Now consider Y no longer to be money but a commodity, as is X. We have then all the following expressions negative :
$$_1U_{\xi_2\xi_2} = {_1V_{yy}}, \qquad _1U_{\xi_1\xi_1} = {_1V_{xx}}, \qquad _2U_{\xi_1\xi_1} = {_2V_{xx}}, \qquad _2U_{\xi_2\xi_2} = {_2V_{yy}}.$$

If in the figure (p. 5) we regard $z = 0$, $z = 1$, ... as contour lines, they indicate the surface or hill $z = {_1V(x, y)}$. Ascent of this hill in any fixed direction between east and south starting from A's zero indifference curve becomes less and less steep till the summit in that direction is reached. Similarly B's surface becomes less steep as one travels from his zero indifference curve in a direction between north and west.

These conditions hold generally, but further complications are found when we take into account possible relations between the uses of X and of Y. These are considered, together with some more general aspects of the utility functions, in the following section, which may be postponed till the more elementary and fundamental analyses in the subsequent chapters have been read.

ADDENDUM.   THE UTILITY SURFACE.

Independent, complementary, and alternative utility.

The shape and properties of the utility surface relating to the interchange of two commodities depend in part on the question whether the uses of the two commodities are independent or correlated. Here the discussion is of a theoretical nature ; the more practical aspects, when both commodities are being purchased by a third person, are considered in chapter VI.

Only A's surface is considered and the prefix 1 is dropped. A's offer is $x \,.\, V_x + y \,.\, V_y = 0$, A giving y in return for x. In this curve

$$D_x y = - D_x (x \,.\, V_x + y \,.\, V_y) \div D_y (x \,.\, V_x + y \,.\, V_y) *$$
$$\qquad y \text{ const.} \qquad\qquad x \text{ const.}$$

$$= - \frac{V_x + x \,.\, V_{xx} + y \,.\, V_{yx}}{x V_{xy} + V_y + y \,.\, V_{yy}},$$

and if $\qquad\qquad p = y/x$, then $y - px = 0$,

and $\therefore \qquad\qquad D_x y - p - x D_x p = 0.$

Eliminate $D_x y$, and simplify. We obtain

$$D_x p = \frac{- V_{xx} \,.\, (V_y)^2 + 2\, V_{xy} \,.\, V_x \,.\, V_y - V_{yy} \,.\, (V_x)^2}{V_y^2 (x \,.\, V_{xy} + V_y + y \,.\, V_{yy})}.$$

Here use the third postulate of p. 2 ; then V_{xx} and V_{yy} are negative. V_x is positive so long as A is not satiated with X, and V_y is negative if A has any use for Y.

$D_x p$ is the gradient of A's demand curve.

V_{xy} is zero if X and Y have completely *independent* uses, so that a change in y does not affect the marginal utility of x, i.e. V_x. In this case $D_x p$ is always negative.

V_{xy} is negative where X and Y have joint or complementary utility, where an increased parting with Y (i. e. an increase of y and a diminution of ξ_2) diminishes the marginal utility of X (e.g. paper and ink). In this case also, $D_x p$ is always negative.

V_{xy} is positive where X and Y are alternative to each other (e.g. bread and meat) and an increase of y (a diminution of ξ_2) increases the marginal utility of x. In this case the sign of $D_x p$ is not determinate. It can be shown that, if

$$- V_y (V_x \,.\, V_{xy} - V_y \,.\, V_{xx}) > V_x (- V_x \,.\, V_{yy} + V_y \,.\, V_{xy}) > 0,$$

$D_x p$ is positive. This will happen if the marginal utility of X changes slowly as x changes, but rapidly as y changes, while V_y changes very rapidly as y changes.

* See Appendix, p. 92.

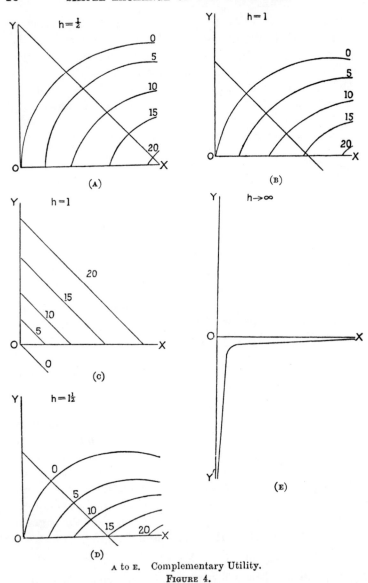

A to E.   Complementary Utility.

FIGURE 4.

For some purposes the utility surface may be considered to be a conicoid with sufficient approximation, without implying that this is the general form. We may then write its equation in the form

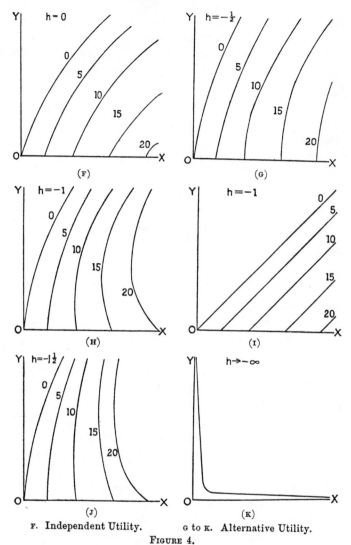

F. Independent Utility.   G to K. Alternative Utility.

FIGURE 4.

$$z = V(x_0 + x, y_0 + y)$$
$$= V(x_0, y_0) + x V_{x_0} + y V_{y_0} + \tfrac{1}{2}x^2 V_{x_0 x_0} + xy V_{x_0 y_0} + \tfrac{1}{2}y^2 V_{y_0 y_0},*$$

where $V_{x_0 x_0}$ stands for the result of writing x_0 for x and y_0 for y in the second partial derivative of V with respect to x, - &c.

* See Appendix, p. 91.

Here the products of cubes of x (the distance from the starting point) and third derived functions are neglected.

Paying regard to the known signs of the differentials, we may write $V_{x_0} = 2g$, $V_{y_0} = -2f$, $V_{x_0 x_0} = -2a$, $V_{y_0 y_0} = -2b$, where $a, b, f,$ and g are positive.

Write $V_{x_0 y_0} = -2h$. h is zero if X and Y are independent, positive if their uses are complementary, negative if they are alternative.

Measure utility as above a zero level at which x_0, y_0 are the quantities possessed.

We have $z = -(ax^2 + 2hxy + by^2) + 2gx - 2fy.$

A's offer curve is
$$ax^2 + 2hxy + by^2 - gx + fy = 0,$$
and his demand curve
$$bp^2 x + 2hpx + fp + ax - g = 0.$$

Independence. The indifference curves are similar and concentric ellipses, which become circles if $a = b$. Figure 4, F (p. 17).

In the sequel take $a = b = 1$ by a suitable choice of units.

Complementary uses. The indifference curves take the shapes of Figures 4, A to E as h increases from zero. When $h = 1$ they are parabolae.* If also $f = -g$, $z = -(x+y)^2 + 2g(x+y)$, Figure 4, C and in any one indifference curve $x+y$ is constant and $p = -1$.

Such a case would arise if a landowner was paying for buildings on part of his estate by giving parcels of land, and reached a point at which he would only *accept* further buildings if land were given back with them.

If $h < 1$, we have ellipses; if $h > 1$, hyperbolae.

Alternative uses. As h diminishes from 0 to $-\infty$, the curves take the forms of Figure 4, G to K. When $0 > h > -1$, the curves are ellipses, when $h < -1$, hyperbolae, when $h = -1$, parabolae. If, when $h = -1$, $f = g$, we have straight lines as in Figure 4, I ; $x - y$ is then constant, and $p = 1$. This occurs when it is completely indifferent to A whether he has X or Y.

* The figures are drawn from the equation $z = -x^2 - 2hxy - y^2 + 10x - 2y$, except Figures 4, C and I where the coefficient of y is taken as 10 and as -10 respectively.

II

MULTIPLE EXCHANGE

§ 1. **Notation.**

It is not difficult to extend the principal results of the first chapter to any number of persons and commodities. In this part of the analysis the first essential is to make sure that the conditions supposed are sufficient to give a determinate solution and that no condition is redundant. This chapter is devoted to the exhibition of these conditions without any reference to the cost of production. We assume that persons have in fact quantities of commodities, of which one may be money, which they are willing to exchange with each other.

Let there be m commodities called X_1, $X_2 \ldots X_r \ldots X_m$, and n persons, A, B, $C \ldots$, shown by prefixes 1, 2, 3... to the quantities and functions related to them.

We shall regard the tth person and the rth commodity as typical, where t stands for any number 1 to n, and r for any number 1 to m.

Suppose that the tth person starts with $_t a_r$ units of X_r, and after exchange has $_t \xi_r = {_t a_r} + {_t x_r}$. $_t x_r$ is positive if he is receiving and negative if he is giving, the symbol involving the necessary sign.

[In Chapter I A was giving a positive quantity y; this would now be written $_1 x_2 = -y$; the other letters correspond as follows: $_2 x_2 = y$, $_1 x_1 = -{_2 x_1} = x$, $_1 a_1 = a_1$, $_1 a_2 = a_2$, $_2 a_1 = b_1$, $_2 a_2 = b_2$.]

Let $p_1 : p_2 : \ldots p_r : \ldots : p_m$ be the price-ratios at which all the exchanges between X_1, $X_2 \ldots$ are made. If X_m is money, $p_m = 1$, and p_1, p_2, &c. are money prices.

We have then to determine $m \times n$ quantities such as $_t x_r$, and $m - 1$ price-ratios.

Let $_t U \left({_t \xi_1}, \ldots {_t \xi_r} \ldots {_t \xi_m} \right)$ be the utility to the tth person of possession or consumption of $_t \xi_1$ of X_1, $\ldots {_t \xi_r}$ of $X_r \ldots {_t \xi_m}$ of X_m.

Write $_tU_r$ for the partial derivative of $_tU$ with respect to ξ_r. $_tU_r$ is then the marginal utility of an increase in the possession of the commodity X_r when $_t\xi_1...\,_t\xi_r...\,_t\xi_m$ are already possessed; it depends in general not only on $_t\xi_r$ but also on the amounts of the other commodities.

Then if $\delta\left(_tU\right)$ is the increment of utility due to exchanges resulting in increments of $...\delta\left(_t\xi_r\right)$ of $X_r...$, we have

$$\delta\left(_tU\right) = {}_tU_1 \cdot \delta\left(_t\xi_1\right) + ... + {}_tU_r \cdot \delta\left(_t\xi_r\right) + ... + {}_tU_m \cdot \delta\left(_t\xi_m\right) *$$
$$= {}_tU_1 \cdot \delta\left(_tx_1\right) + ... + {}_tU_r \cdot \delta\left(_tx_r\right) + ... + {}_tU_m \cdot \delta\left(_tx_m\right),$$

since $_t\xi_r = {}_ta_r + {}_tx_r$ and therefore $\delta\left(_t\xi_r\right) = \delta\left(_tx_r\right)$, &c.

We must now distinguish between two cases, that of competition or the open market and that of monopoly.

§ 2. Equations of equilibrium for perfect competition.

Any two persons A and B interchange quantities of any two commodities X_1 and X_2 in quantities so small relatively to the whole amounts exchanged by all persons that their exchange does not significantly affect the price-ratios, which are therefore not subject to variation in the process of differentiation. The price-ratios are the same for all persons. This is the condition of the open market.

Writing the last equation for this case, only x_1 and x_2 varying, we have
$$\delta\left(_1U\right) = {}_1U_1 \cdot \delta\left(_1x_1\right) + {}_1U_2 \cdot \delta\left(_1x_2\right)$$
and
$$\delta\left(_2U\right) = {}_2U_1 \cdot \delta\left(_2x_1\right) + {}_2U_2 \cdot \delta\left(_2x_2\right).$$

As in Chapter I exchanges will be pushed till both A's and B's utility is maximized, at which position $\delta\left(_1U\right) = 0 = \delta\left(_2U\right)$,

$$\therefore \; {}_1U_1 \cdot \delta\left(_1x_1\right) + {}_1U_2 \cdot \delta\left(_1x_2\right) = 0 = {}_2U_1 \cdot \delta\left(_2x_1\right) + {}_2U_2 \cdot \delta\left(_2x_2\right).$$

Also for both persons the sum spent equals the sum received,

$$\therefore \; p_1 \cdot {}_1x_1 + p_2 \cdot {}_1x_2 = 0 \text{ and } p_1 \cdot {}_2x_1 + p_2 \cdot {}_2x_2 = 0,$$
whence
$$p_1 \cdot \delta\left(_1x_1\right) + p_2 \cdot \delta\left(_1x_2\right) = 0 = p_1 \cdot \delta\left(_2x_1\right) + p_2 \cdot \delta\left(_2x_2\right).$$

From these equations eliminate the quantities $\delta\left(_1x_1\right)$, &c., and we obtain

$$\frac{1}{p_1} \cdot {}_1U_1 = \frac{1}{p_2} \cdot {}_1U_2 \quad \text{and} \quad \frac{1}{p_1} \cdot {}_2U_1 = \frac{1}{p_2} \cdot {}_2U_2.$$

* See Appendix, p. 90.

These equations are of the same form as in Chapter I, but now the values of $_1U_1$, &c., depend not only on the two commodities exchanged but also on the amount of all commodities possessed.

Writing similar equations for all exchanges we have

Maximizing equations

$$\frac{1}{p_1} \cdot {}_tU_1 = \dots = \frac{1}{p_r} \cdot {}_tU_r = \dots = \frac{1}{p_m} {}_tU_m \quad\Big|\quad (m-1)\, n \text{ equations.}$$
$$\text{for } t = 1, 2 \dots n \quad\Big|$$

Thus at the position at which the exchanges are completed the quantity $\dfrac{1}{p_r} \cdot {}_tU_r$ is the same for all commodities to the same person, and equals $_tU_m$, the marginal utility of money, if X_m is money. In simple words, in spending money the greatest satisfaction is obtained when the transference of a trifling sum from one purchase to another would have an insignificant effect on satisfaction. If sugar (X_1) is 8*d*. a lb. and butter (X_2) 2*s*. a lb., so that $p_1 : p_2 = 1 : 3$, then at the final purchase the utility of a $\frac{1}{4}$ lb. of sugar is one-third of the utility of a $\frac{1}{4}$ lb. of butter, and $_tU_1 = \frac{1}{3} \cdot {}_tU_2$. 2*d*. gives the same satisfaction spent either way.

We have two sets of quantitative equations to complete the solution. For each commodity the amount bought equals the amount sold. Hence

Commodity equations

$$\sum_{t=1}^{t=n} {}_tx_r = 0 * \text{ for } r = 1, 2 \dots m \quad\Big|\quad m \text{ equations.}$$

Again the sum spent by each person equals the sum received. Hence

Personal equations

$$\sum_{r=1}^{r=m} p_r \cdot {}_tx_r = 0 \text{ for } t = 1, 2 \dots n \quad\Big|\quad n \text{ equations.}$$

But the sum of the commodity equations, multiplied by p_1, p_2, &c., and that of the personal equations both give $\Sigma p_r \cdot {}_tx_r = 0$, the summation extending over the $m \times n$ terms,

---

* This equation is the abbreviation of $_tx_1 + {}_tx_2 + \dots + {}_tx_n = 0$.

and therefore one of these $\overline{m+n}$ equations is deducible from the others.

We have then $m+n-1$ equations to combine with the $(m-1)n$ maximizing equations, that is $mn+m-1$ equations in all. These are just sufficient to determine * the mn quantities $_tx_r$ and $m-1$ price-ratios, or, if X_m represents money, $\overline{m-1}$ prices.†

An important corollary is that every person can maximize his satisfaction at the same time.

§ 3. Equations of equilibrium for monopoly.

Suppose now that A produces all of X_1 or so much that he can influence the price, and consider his dealings with B who cannot affect prices when exchanging X_2 for X_1. Write $p = p_1/p_2$.

For B as in the case of competition we have

$$p = {}_2U_1/{}_2U_2 = -x_2/x_1,$$

where $-x_2$ is the quantity of X_2 that B gives in return for x_1 of X_1.‡ ${}_2U_1$ and ${}_2U_2$, either or both, involve x_2, so that x_2 can be eliminated from the two equations and p obtained as a function of x_1, say $p = f(x_1)$ the form already used for a demand curve.

A maximizes ${}_1U$, so that as before

$$0 = \delta_1U = {}_1U_1\delta x_1 + {}_1U_2\delta x_2. \,\S$$

Also $p \,.\, x_1 + x_2 = 0$, but now p varies and the equation of variation $\delta(p \,.\, x_1) + \delta(x_2) = 0$ does not reduce to $p\delta(x_1) + \delta(x_2) = 0$, but to

$$\delta\{x_1 f(x_1)\} + \delta x_2 = 0,$$

i. e.

$$\{f(x_1) + x_1 f'(x_1)\}\delta x_1 + \delta x_2 = 0.$$

Hence the competitive equation

$$\frac{1}{p_1} \,.\, {}_1U_1 = \frac{1}{p_2} \,.\, {}_1U_2$$

is replaced by the equation

$$\frac{{}_1U_1}{f(x_1) + x_1 f'(x_1)} = {}_1U_2.$$

---

* See Appendix, p. 94.

† Actually multiple solutions each giving a set of values of $_tx_r$, &c., are possible, but only one set is likely to be applicable to known conditions.

‡ $x_2 = {}_2x_2 = -{}_1x_2$, and $x_1 = -{}_1x_1 = {}_2x_1$.

§ See Appendix, pp. 89-91.

Since $f(x_1) + x_1 f'(x_1) = D_{x_1}(px_1) = -D_{x_1}(x_2)$,
the differentiation being performed on the curve

$$x_1 \cdot {}_2U_1 + x_2 \cdot {}_2U_2 = 0,$$

we may write this equation

$$_1U_1 + {}_1U_2 \cdot D_{x1}(x_2) = 0.$$

In fact $D_{x_1}(x_2)$ is the gradient of B's offer curve, and $_1U_1/_1U_2$ is the gradient of A's indifference curve, so that the condition is that B's offer curve touches one of A's indifference curves, as at Q_2 in Figure 1 (p. 5).* Equilibrium is at Q_2 instead of at Q. But that figure and the analysis in Chapter I assume the existence of only two commodities, while the functions in the equations just used include quantities of X_3, X_4 ... as well, though these are not supposed to vary during the exchange between A and B of X_1 and X_2.

If A has no use for X_1 himself, or his use is satiated, $_1U_1 = 0$ and the equation becomes $D_{x_1}(x_2) = 0$.

In this case x_2 is a maximum in B's offer curve, as is illustrated in the accompanying figure. The horizontal lines are A's indifference lines which depend solely on x_2. A chooses the highest possible point on B's offer curve (where $D_{x_1}(x_2) = 0$), that is where it touches an indifference line, as at Q in the figure. $OM = x_1$, $MQ = x_2$, and QM/OM is the price of x_1 in terms of x_2.

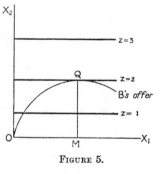

FIGURE 5.

If there are only two commodities and B has the monopoly of the second the position is indeterminate without further information, for example of the relative strength of A's and B's positions in bargaining. In the figure on p. 5 the bargainers aim respectively at Q_1 and Q_2. In the figure here given B's indifference lines would be vertical and A's and B's offer curves

---

* But in that figure it must be supposed that A is monopolist of y, and forcing B to give him x on favourable terms, since there he is paying with Y and buying X. In the analysis just given A is paying with X_1 and buying X_2.

indeterminate; A would try to push B up the OX_2 scale, and B to push A to the right. A possible equilibrium is when they were on the summit of the hill indicated if the indifference lines are contours, where they would both reach satiety.

If there are many commodities, A still monopolizing the first, write A's equations

$$_1U_1 \cdot \delta\,(_1r_1) + {}_1U_2\delta\,(_1x_2) + \ldots = 0$$
$$p_1 \cdot {}_1x_1 + p_2 \cdot {}_1x_2 + \ldots \qquad = 0$$
$$\delta\,(p_1 \cdot {}_1x_1) + p_2 \cdot \delta\,(_1x_2)\ldots \qquad = 0$$

Since as in competition

$$\frac{1}{p_2} \cdot {}_1U_2 = \frac{1}{p_3} \cdot {}_1U_3 = \ldots,$$

and $\qquad \delta\,(p_1 \cdot {}_1x_1) = D_{x_1}(p_1 \cdot {}_1x_1) \cdot \delta\,(_1x_1)$

we have $\qquad \dfrac{_1U_1}{D_{x_1}(p_1 \cdot {}_1x_1)} = \dfrac{1}{p_2} \cdot {}_1U_2 = \dfrac{1}{p_3} \cdot {}_1U_3 = \ldots,$

where p_1 is connected with x_1 by the aggregate demand for X_1 of B, C... (see p. 25).

Then, if also B monopolizes X_2, C X_3, and so on, in the maximizing equations $\qquad \dfrac{1}{p_2} \cdot {}_2U_2, \quad \dfrac{1}{p_3} \cdot {}_3U_3 \ldots$

are replaced by $\qquad \dfrac{_2U_2}{D_{x_2}(p_2 \cdot {}_2x_2)}, \quad \dfrac{_3U_3}{D_{x_3}(p_3 \cdot {}_3x_3)} \ldots ;$

but this process must stop before the last commodity is monopolized, for it is found that as in the case of two persons and two commodities the problem becomes indeterminate when there is no unmonopolized commodity. The final p_m cannot be expressed as a function of x_m.

It should be noticed in this case and in all cases of maxima, that the change in the quantity maximized is very slow as the variable moves away from the position that gives the maximum. For example, in the figure on p. 23, A will lose little of X_2 if he gives perceptibly more of X_1, moving M to the right.

More generally A receives, say, $R\,(x_1) = x_1 f(x_1)$, where $f(x_1) = p$, the price at x_1 from the demand curve.

Let $\bar{x}$ be the value of x_1 that makes $R(x_1)$ a maximum, so that $f(\bar{x}) + \bar{x}f'(\bar{x}) = 0$, and let $\bar{x} + h$ be a neighbouring value.
Then

$$R(\bar{x} + h) - R(\bar{x})$$
$$= (\bar{x} + h) \cdot f(\bar{x} + h) - \bar{x}f(\bar{x})$$
$$= (\bar{x} + h)\{f(\bar{x}) + h \cdot f'(\bar{x}) + \tfrac{1}{2}h^2 \cdot f''(\bar{x}) + \ldots\}* - \bar{x}f(\bar{x})$$
$$= h\{f(\bar{x}) + \bar{x} \cdot f'(\bar{x})\} + h^2 \cdot f'(\bar{x}) + \tfrac{1}{2}h^2(\bar{x} + h)f''(\bar{x}) + \ldots$$
$$= h^2f'(\bar{x}) + \tfrac{1}{2}h^2(\bar{x} + h)f''(\bar{x}) + \ldots$$

The increase in p is

$$f(\bar{x} + h) - f(\bar{x}) = hf'(\bar{x}) + \tfrac{1}{2}h^2f''(\bar{x}) + \ldots$$

Write $h = \lambda\bar{x}$, neglect terms involving λ^3, and for simplicity suppose $f''(\bar{x})$, the change of the direction of the demand curve, to be small so that we can neglect also $\lambda^2f''(\bar{x})$.

Write $-\delta R$, $-\delta p$ for the changes in R, p. Then

$$\frac{\delta R}{R} = -\frac{\lambda^2\bar{x}\,^2 f'(\bar{x})}{\bar{x}f(\bar{x})} = \lambda^2 \quad \text{and} \quad \frac{\delta p}{p} = -\frac{\lambda\bar{x}f'(\bar{x})}{f(\bar{x})} = \lambda,$$

so that approximately the relative decrease in the price equals the relative increase (λ) in the quantity received by the purchaser, while the relative decrease in the amount received by the monopolist equals the square of λ. If, then, the decrease of price is 10 % ($\lambda = 0.1$) the increase in x_1 is approximately 10 %, but the decrease in R is only about 1 %. A monopolist may often find it to his ultimate advantage to encourage his customers by not exacting the uttermost farthing.

§ 4. Aggregate demand and supply.

Let x_r be the sum of those of the quantities $_1x_r, _2x_r \ldots$ that are positive, that is of the amounts that are bought; then $-x_r$ is the sum of the remaining negative quantities, the amounts that are sold.

Let there be n' purchasers, where n' is of course less than n. The n' quantities of which $_tx_r$ is typical are connected by the equations $\qquad x_r = {}_1x_r + \ldots + {}_tx_r + \ldots {}_{n'}x_r,$

$$\frac{p_r}{p_m} = \frac{{}_1U_r}{{}_1U_m} = \ldots = \frac{{}_tU_r}{{}_tU_m} = \ldots \frac{{}_{n'}U_r}{{}_{n'}U_m},$$

* See Appendix, p. 84.

where we may suppose for simplicity the terms in the denominator to depend on money, so that $p_m = 1$ and $_tU_m$ is the marginal utility of money to the tth person. We have $n' + 1$ equations, from which the n' quantities such as $_t x_r$ can be eliminated, leaving a relation between p_r, x_r and prices and quantities of commodities other than the rth. This may be written $p_r = f(x_r)$, where, though the function involves other commodities, we can study the change in p_r due to a change in x_r (by the method of partial differentiation, for example) on the hypothesis that other prices and quantities remain constant, or are affected so little that they may be regarded as constant. This is the aggregate demand equation for X_r, which may be considered by the analysis used on pp. 9–12 above. The elasticity at any point on it, depending only on the value of p_r and the direction of the curve at that point, is not affected by any ordinary corresponding changes in the other quantities.

An aggregate supply equation can be obtained in the same way, but supply is better studied in relation to production as in the following chapters.

NOTE. *On universal monopoly.*

Consider the case of three monopolists A, B, C and three commodities, and one other person D. Let A monopolize X_1, B X_2, and C X_3, producing x_1, x_2, and x_3 respectively, and let D possess, but not monopolize X_4. Then

$$\left.\begin{array}{l} x_1 = -_2x_1 -_3x_1 -_4x_1 \\ x_2 = -_1x_2 -_3x_2 -_4x_2 \\ x_3 = -_1x_3 -_2x_3 -_4x_3 \\ _4x_4 = -_1x_4 -_2x_4 -_3x_4 \end{array}\right\} \quad \dots \quad \text{(i)}$$

where x_1, x_2, x_3 are written for $_1x_1$, $_2x_2$, and $_3x_3$,

$$\left.\begin{array}{l} p_1 \cdot x_1 + p_2 \cdot _1x_2 + p_3 \cdot _1x_3 + p_4 \cdot _1x_4 = 0 \\ p_1 \cdot _2x_1 + p_2 \cdot x_2 + p_3 \cdot _2x_3 + p_4 \cdot _2x_4 = 0 \\ p_1 \cdot _3x_1 + p_2 \cdot _3x_2 + p_3 \cdot x_3 + p_4 \cdot _3x_4 = 0 \end{array}\right\} \quad \dots \quad \text{(ii)}$$

$$\frac{_1U_1}{D_{x_1}(p_1x_1)} = \frac{_1U_2}{p_2} = \frac{_1U_3}{p_3} = \frac{_1U_4}{p_4} \quad \dots \quad \text{(iii)}$$

$$\frac{_2U_1}{p_1} = \frac{_2U_2}{D_{x_2}(p_2x_2)} = \frac{_2U_3}{p_3} = \frac{_2U_4}{p_4} \quad \dots \quad \text{(iv)}$$

$$\frac{_3U_1}{p_1} = \frac{_3U_2}{p_2} = \frac{_3U_3}{D_{x_3}(p_3x_3)} = \frac{_3U_4}{p_4} \quad \cdots \cdots \quad \text{(v)}$$

$$\frac{_4U_1}{p_1} = \frac{_4U_2}{p_2} = \frac{_4U_3}{p_3} = \frac{_4U_4}{p_4} \quad \cdots \cdots \quad \text{(vi)}$$

We have nineteen equations to determine sixteen x's and three price ratios. Set aside the terms containing the differential in (iii), (iv), and (v), and also the first equation of (v). From the remaining fifteen equations eliminate* p_4 and thirteen x's (all but x_1, x_2, x_3), and so obtain p_1 as a function of x_1, x_2, x_3, p_2, and p_3; then keeping x_2, x_3, p_2 and p_3 constant we can obtain $D_x(p_1)$. Then the first equations of (iii) and of (v) enable us to eliminate p_1 and x_1.

We have now eliminated fifteen quantities and have left x_2, x_3, p_2, and p_3 connected by the three equations

$$\frac{_2U_2}{D_{x_2}(p_2x_2)} = \frac{_2U_3}{p_3}, \quad \frac{_3U_1}{p_1} = \frac{_3U_2}{p_2}, \quad \frac{_3U_2}{p_2} = \frac{_3U_3}{D_{x_3}(p_3x_3)}$$

in whatever form they take after the eliminations.

From the middle equation express p_2 as a function of x_2, x_3, and p_3, and differentiate the equation so found to obtain $D_{x_2}(p_2)$. Then from the first and middle equations we can express x_2 and p_2 each in terms of x_3 and p_3; but we cannot connect p_3 and x_3 and therefore cannot differentiate p_3, which is necessary to complete the solution.

If, however, the last denominator were p_3, as it would be if C had not monopolized X_3, the last-named three equations would involve the three quantities x_2, x_3, and p_2/p_3, which could be found; or we could have simplified the whole analysis by writing $p_3 = 1$.

The analysis can be extended so as to include more commodities.

It is not of course denied that exchange would take place if all the commodities were monopolized, but it is shown that further information is necessary to determine the amounts exchanged.

* See Appendix, p. 94.

III

PRODUCTION

§ 1. Factors of production.

The indifference curves of a person supplying commodities are not decided, except very rarely, by the utility of them to himself, but by their cost of production.

Let the production of X_1, X_2 ... X_m depend on the use of such *factors of production* as capital, labour, and materials, v in number, which we will call $Y_1 ... Y_s ... Y_v$, Y_s being regarded as typical.

We shall have to consider later the laws that govern the supply and price of the factors. At present suppose that a producer can obtain as much as he pleases of each factor at an unvarying price which he cannot influence.

Any factor is to be regarded as usable in the production of any commodity. It will be found throughout that when one is not used a corresponding equation drops out.

The quantity of a factor used for a given quantity of production is not fixed, but the increased use of one factor and decreased use of others may leave the production unchanged.

We have to discover the mathematical formulae which measure the amounts of the different factors used in the production of one commodity, and the relative amounts of one factor used in the production of different commodities. We have further to determine the distribution of each factor among different manufacturers of one commodity.

§ 2. The law of substitution.

Joint demand for factors.

First let there be only one commodity and only one producer or manufacturer.

Let $y_1 ... y_s ... y_v$ be quantities of the factors (such as y_1 hours of labour, the use of y_2 acres of land, and of £100y_3 worth of capital) used in the production of x units of the commodity.

The quantity x depends, in a way that is presumed to be known, on $...y_s...$, so that we may write

$$x = F(y_1...y_s...y_\nu)$$

where F is a function of given form.

Let $\pi_1...\pi_s...\pi$ be the prices per unit of $Y_1...Y_s...Y_\nu$, supposed given.

Let $p'x$ be the cost of production of the x units.*

The manufacturer's aim is so to choose the quantities such as y_s as to minimize p'. The resulting organization of production may depend on the magnitude of x, and the problem must be solved for each value of x, which is therefore kept constant in the solution.

We have $\quad p'x = \pi_1 y_1 + ... + \pi_s y_s + ... + \pi_\nu y_\nu.$

$$\therefore \; \delta(p'x) = x \cdot \delta p' = \pi_1 \cdot \delta y_1 + ... + \pi_s \cdot \delta y_s + ... + \pi_\nu \cdot \delta y_\nu.$$

Also since x does not vary

$$0 = \delta x = F_{y_1} \cdot \delta y_1 + ... + F_{y_s} \cdot \delta y_s + ... + F_{y_\nu} \cdot \delta y_\nu,†$$

where F_{y_s} is the partial derivative of F with respect to y_s. Eliminate δy_1.

$$x \cdot \delta p' = \frac{1}{F_{y_1}} \{(\pi_2 \cdot F_{y_1} - \pi_1 \cdot F_{y_2}) \delta y_2 + ...$$
$$+ (\pi_s \cdot F_{y_1} - \pi_1 \cdot F_{y_s}) \delta y_s + ...\}.$$

When p' is a minimum $\delta p' = 0$ for all possible small variations of $...y_s....†$ In the last equation $\delta y_2 ... \delta y_s ...$ are independent of each other, and the solution is obtained by putting each coefficient equal to zero.

Then $\quad\quad \pi_s \cdot F_{y_1} = \pi_1 \cdot F_{y_s},$

and $\quad \dfrac{1}{\pi_1} \cdot F_{y_1} = ... = \dfrac{1}{\pi_s} \cdot F_{y_s} = ... = \dfrac{1}{\pi_\nu} F_{y_\nu}.$

This is the law of substitution, which determines the amount of the factors used in the production of a commodity. In words, at the cheapest cost of production the rate of increment in the

* The letters with ′ always relate to production or supply and the corresponding letters without to consumption or demand. For a tabular statement of the complete notation, see p. 46.

† See Appendix, pp. 89, 90.

amount produced by varying one factor alone (or the marginal increment) is proportional to the price per unit of that factor. A consequence is that at the minimum the transfer of a small sum from expenditure on one factor to expenditure on any other leaves the price of production unchanged. (Compare the corresponding statement relating to expenditure on commodities, p. 21.)

[For example, take
$$x = F(y_1, y_2) = 2y_1^2 + 3y_1y_2, \text{ and } \pi_1 = 2, \pi_2 = 1.$$
Then $p'x = 2y_1 + y_2,\ F_{y_1} = 4y_1 + 3y_2,\ F_{y_2} = 3y_1.$
The solution for $x = 10$, say, is obtained from the equations
$$2y_1^2 + 3y_1y_2 = 10,\ \tfrac{1}{2}(4y_1 + 3y_2) = 3y_1,$$
whence $y_1 = 1{\cdot}6,\ y_2 = 1{\cdot}05,\ p' = 0{\cdot}42.$

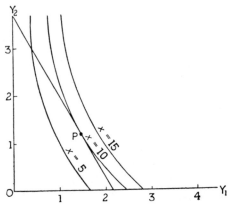

FIGURE 6.   Production Diagram.

Geometrically (y_1, y_2) is the point P, where a tangent * parallel to $\pi_1 y_1 + \pi_2 y_2 = 2y_1 + y_2 = $ const. touches $F(y_1, y_2) = 10$.]

§ 3. The supply curve.

The $\nu + 1$ equations, $x = F(y_1 \ldots y_s \ldots y_\nu)$
$$p'x = \pi_1\, y + \ldots + \pi_s y_s + \ldots + \pi_\nu \mathit{y}_\nu$$
$$\frac{1}{\pi_1} F_{y_1} = \ldots = \frac{1}{\pi_s} F_{y_s} = \ldots = \frac{1}{\pi_\nu} \cdot F_{y_\nu},$$

* See Appendix, p. 92.

are sufficient to eliminate the v terms such as y_s and to give p' as a function of x, say $p' = \phi(x)$.

This is the supply curve for X.

If $\qquad x = F = a_1 y_1 + \ldots + a_s y_s + \ldots + a_v y_v,$

so that $F_{y_s} = a_s$, &c., the solution breaks down. In this case

$$p' = \frac{\pi_1 y_1 + \ldots + \pi_s y_s + \ldots + \pi_v y_v}{a_1 y_1 + \ldots + a_s y_s + \ldots + a_v y_v},$$

so that p' may be anywhere between the greatest and the least of such terms as π/a. If π_1/a_1 is the least, p' is a minimum when only Y_1 is used. This is the extreme case of *alternative* factors.

On the other hand, if Y_1 and Y_2 are only usable *jointly* in the proportion $a_1 : a_2$, we may write $a_1 y_1 + a_2 y_2 = a'y'$, and replace

$$\frac{1}{\pi_1} \cdot F_{y_1} = \frac{1}{\pi_2} \cdot F_{y_2} = \ldots \quad \text{by} \quad \frac{a'}{\pi_1 a_1 + \pi_2 a_2} \cdot F_{y'} = \ldots,$$

still having sufficient equations.

§ 4. The integral supply curve.

Write $\mu = p'x$, the cost of x units of X.

Then $\mu = x\phi(x) = \chi(x)$, say.

$\mu = \chi(x)$ is the producer's offer curve, and may be called the *integral supply curve* (Fig. 7), to distinguish it from $p' = \phi(x)$ which is called simply the supply curve (Fig. 8).

[e.g. in the above example
$$\mu = p'x = p'(2y_1^2 + 3y_1 y_2)$$
$$= 2y_1 + 1 \cdot y_2$$
and $\qquad \frac{1}{2}(4y_1 + 3y_2) = 3y_1.$

Eliminate y_1 and y_2 and we have

$$\mu = \frac{4}{3}\sqrt{x},$$

the integral supply curve; and

$$p' = \frac{4}{3\sqrt{x}},$$

the supply curve.]

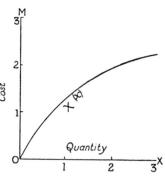

FIGURE 7.   Integral Supply Curve.

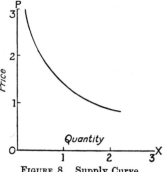

FIGURE 8.   Supply Curve.

§ 5. Elasticity of supply.

It is evidently important to analyse the relationship between changes in the quantity produced and the expense of producing them. For this purpose we may use either μ or p'.

Write
$$e = -\frac{p'}{\delta p'} \div \frac{x}{\delta x},$$

where δx a small increment of x is connected with $-\delta p'$ a small decrement of p', or proceeding to the limit, write

$$e = -\frac{p'}{x D_x p'} = \frac{\phi(x)}{-x \phi'(x)}.$$

e is the *elasticity of supply*, corresponding with η the elasticity of demand. It is generally written with the negative sign, so that it is a positive quantity when $\phi'(x)$ is negative.

Write $\epsilon = \mu/x D_x \mu$, so that ϵ measures the ratio of the relative increase of cost to the relative increase of output, while e measures the ratio of the relative decrease of price to the relative increase of output. "$\epsilon \gtreqless 1$ according as the expense of producing $[x]$ involves what may be called increasing, constant, or diminishing efficiency of money." *

ϵ has an interesting connexion with the marginal contributions (F_{y_s}) of the factors to the production.

Write $\dfrac{1}{\pi_1} \cdot F_{y_1} = \ldots = \dfrac{1}{\pi_s} \cdot F_{y_s} = \ldots = \dfrac{1}{\pi_\nu} \cdot F_{y_\nu} = k.$

In the curve $\mu = \chi(x)$

$$D_x \mu = \mathop{\mathrm{L}}\limits^{t} \frac{\delta \mu}{\delta x} = \mathop{\mathrm{L}}\limits^{t} \frac{\pi . \delta y_1 + \ldots + \pi_s \delta y_s + \ldots}{F_{y_1} . \delta y_1 + \ldots + F_{y_s} . \delta y_s + \ldots} = \frac{1}{k}.$$

$$\therefore \; \epsilon = \mu k/x = (\pi_1 y_1 + \ldots + \pi_s y_s + \ldots) \, k/x$$
$$= \frac{y_1}{x} F_{y_1} + \ldots + \frac{y_s}{x} F_{y_s} + \ldots + \frac{y_\nu}{x} F_{y_\nu}.$$

Also, since $\mu = p'x$, $\epsilon = kp'$.

---

* This term is used by Mr. W. E. Johnson, *Economic Journal*, 1913, pp. 507 sqq.

The relation between e and ϵ is a simple one.

$$D_x\mu = p' + xD_xp'.$$
$$\therefore \; \mu/\epsilon x = p' - p'/e.$$
$$\therefore \; \frac{1}{e} + \frac{1}{\epsilon} = 1 \; \text{ and } \; e = \frac{\epsilon}{\epsilon - 1}.$$

§ 6. **Increasing, constant, and diminishing (or decreasing) return.**

We have three cases.

Increasing return.

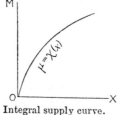 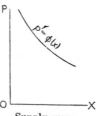

| Integral supply curve. | Supply curve. |

FIGURE 9.

Here $\epsilon > 1$, e is positive and $\phi'(x)$ negative.

The more there is produced, the smaller the supply price. $xD_x\mu - \mu < 0$, and hence by differentiating $xD_x^2\mu < 0$, so that the integral supply curve is concave to the axis of x.

Constant return.

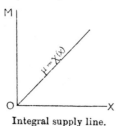 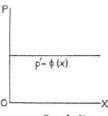

| Integral supply line. | Supply line. |

FIGURE 10.

Here $\epsilon = 1$, e is infinite, $\phi'(x)$ is zero, and the supply curve becomes a horizontal line.

$xD_x\mu - \mu = 0$, $D_x^2\mu = 0$, $D_x\mu$ is constant, and the integral supply curve becomes a straight line through the origin.

Diminishing return.

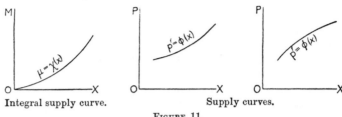

Integral supply curve.   Supply curves.

FIGURE 11.

Here $\epsilon < 1$, e is negative and $\phi'(x)$ is positive.

The more there is produced, the greater the supply price.

$D_x^2\mu$ is positive and the integral supply curve is convex to the axis of x.

§ 7. Marginal supply prices.

The supply price, p', is simply the whole cost of the production of x divided by x. We may obtain another view as follows.

The cost of producing $x + \delta x$, with the organization of factors which minimizes cost at that rate of output, is greater than the cost of producing x under the organization appropriate to x by the quantity $\chi(x + \delta x) - \chi(x)$.

Write

$$p'_m = \Phi(x) = \mathop{\bigsqcup}\limits^{t} \frac{\chi(x + \delta x) - \chi(x)}{\delta x} = \chi'(x) = D_x\mu.$$

Then

$$p'_m = D_x\{x\phi(x)\} = \phi(x) + x\phi'(x) = p' + xD_xp'$$
$$= \phi(x)\left(1 - \frac{1}{e}\right) = \frac{1}{\epsilon}\,\phi(x) = \frac{p'}{\epsilon}.$$

p'_m is a definite function of x, which equals p' in constant return, $> p'$ in diminishing return, and $< p'$ in increasing return.

Also

$$\int_0^x p'_m\, dx = \mu = p'x,$$

so that p' is the average value of p'_m over the region 0 to x.

p'_m is called the marginal supply price, and $p'_m = \Phi(x)$ the curve of marginal supply prices.*

* See Pigou, *Economics of Welfare*, pp. 931 seq.

[p'_m is not the cost of the last unit produced, but the additional cost of producing one more unit *after* adapting the organization of the factors of production.]

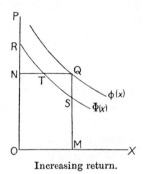
Increasing return.

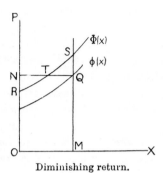
Diminishing return.

FIGURE 12.

In the figures $MQ = p'$, $MS = p'_m$, where OM is the amount produced per unit period.

The area $OMQN = p'x =$ area $OMSR$, and therefore the area $RNT =$ the area TQS.

The following numerical examples may elucidate the relationship of the quantities:

Increasing return.

x (units produced).	μ (whole cost).	p' (average cost).	p'_m (marginal price).
1	20s.	20s.	
2	35s.	$17\frac{1}{2}s.$	$x = 1\frac{1}{2}$ 15s.
3	45s.	15s.	$x = 2\frac{1}{2}$ 10s.
4	50s.	$12\frac{1}{2}s.$	$x = 3\frac{1}{2}$ 5s.

Here $p' = \phi(x) = 22\frac{1}{2} - 2\frac{1}{2}x$, $\phi'(x) = -2\frac{1}{2}$, $p'_m = 22\frac{1}{2} - 5x$.
15s. is the cost of producing two units less the cost of producing one. With such small numbers the continuity is lost.

Diminishing return.

x	μ	p'	p'_m
1	20	20	
2	45	$22\frac{1}{2}$	$x = 1\frac{1}{2}$ 25
3	75	25	$x = 2\frac{1}{2}$ 30
4	110	$72\frac{1}{2}$	$x = 3\frac{1}{2}$ 35

Here $p' = \phi(x) = 17\frac{1}{2} + 2\frac{1}{2}x$, $p'_m = 17\frac{1}{2} + 5x$.

§ 8. Several manufacturers, one commodity.

There is little difficulty in obtaining the equation of the supply curve, when there are several manufacturers of a commodity, who owing to difference in situation or ability combine the factors of production in different ways, indicated by the prefixes before F. (It may be left to the reader to modify the argument to fit the case where the manufacturers use identical methods and similar organizations.)

Let there be n' manufacturers or producers of X, who working under different conditions combine the factors in various ways.

Let $\pi_1...\pi_s...\pi_\nu$ be the same for all producers.

Let the tth manufacturer use amounts $_ty_1..._ty_s..._ty_\nu$ of the factors and produce $_tx$ of X, and let x be their aggregate production.

Then

$$x = {}_1x + ... + {}_tx + ... + {}_{n'}x. \qquad \vdots \;\; \text{1 equation.}$$

$$_tx = {}_tF(y_1...y_s...y_\nu), \text{ for } t = 1...n'. \qquad \vdots \;\; n' \text{ equations.}$$

$$\frac{1}{\pi_1} \cdot {}_tF_{y_1} = ... = \frac{1}{\pi_s} \cdot {}_tF_{y_s} = ... = \frac{1}{\pi_\nu} \cdot {}_tF_{y_\nu}, \qquad \vdots$$
$$\text{for } t = 1...n'. \qquad \vdots \;\; n'(\nu-1) \text{ equations.}$$

where $_ty_1$ is to be written for y_1 in $_tF_{y_1}$, &c., after differentiation.

Let $_tp' \cdot {}_tx$ be the whole cost to the tth producer, so that

$$_tp' \cdot {}_tx = \pi_1 \cdot {}_ty_1 + ... + \pi_s \cdot {}_ty_s + ... + \pi_\nu \cdot {}_ty_\nu, \qquad \vdots$$
$$\text{for } t = 1...n'. \qquad \vdots \;\; n' \text{ equations.}$$

We have now $n'\nu + n' + 1$ equations, and $n'\nu$ quantities such as $_ty_s$ and n' such as $_tx$.

From the $\nu + 1$ equations with prefix t we can eliminate $_ty_1..._ty_\nu$ and obtain $_tp'$ as a function of $_tx$, say,

$$_tp' = {}_t\phi\,({}_tx), \;\; t = 1...n',$$

and combining these n' supply equations with the first equation above express x as a function of $_1p'..._tp'..._{n'}p'$.

We need n' further equations to determine these prices, which depend on the following considerations.

If the producers' supply equations show *constant* or *increasing* return, no equilibrium is in general reached theoretically till one has driven all the others from the market or combined with them.* But increasing may give way to decreasing return when a producer takes on more than he can manage, and in that case (not here analysed) more suppliers than one remain.

With *decreasing* return and competition, when there are many producers and no individual contributes enough to the supply to exert a perceptible influence on the price, each will extend his production till the cost of producing one more unit (after adjustment of factors is allowed for), equals the selling price given by the demand curve $p = f(x)$. That is, if his marginal supply price is ${}_t p'_m$, till

$$_t p'_m = {}_t \phi(x) + {}_t x \phi'(x) = {}_t p' + {}_t x D_x({}_t p') = p = f(x).$$

We have then the n' equations needed, thus

$$f(x) = {}_1 p' + {}_1 x D_x({}_1 p') = \dots = {}_t p' + {}_t x D_x({}_t p') = \dots$$
$$= {}_{n'} p' + {}_{n'} x D_x({}_n p').$$

In the whole problem we have $n' v + 2 n' + 1$ equations, which are just sufficient to determine $n' v$ terms such as ${}_t y_s$, n' as ${}_t x$, n' as ${}_t p'$, and x, in terms of the π's and the constants of the functions.

The tth producer makes a profit $(f(x) - {}_t \phi(x)) \cdot {}_t x$. The relationship of this to rent and surplus generally is discussed in Chapter VII below.

The assumption that an individual cannot affect the selling price requires examination. If the price were momentarily at p, as given by the above equations, the first producer could obtain a greater profit by reducing his production to that given by

$$D_x\{f(x) - {}_1 \phi(x)\} {}_1 x = 0, \quad \text{i. e.} \quad f(x) + {}_1 x f'(x) = {}_1 p'_m,$$

if other producers were not affected. As a result it can be shown that the selling price would increase, and then the other producers would push up their production till the marginal supply price of each equalled the new price. This would cause over-production at the new price, which would therefore fall. The above equations therefore give stable equilibrium, if no producer is predominant.

* See, however, Pigou, *Economics of Welfare*, pp. 439-41.

If there is only one producer, or if they all combine, we have monopoly, which is discussed in Chapter VII, § 3 seq. below.

The case of two producers, 'duopoly', may be illustrated by the following simple example :

Let the demand line be $p = c - k\,(x_1 + x_2)$, and the suppliers' lines $p_1 = l_1 x_1$, $p_2 = l_2 x_2$.

The first supplier varies x_1 to maximize

$$(c - k\,(x_1 + x_2) - l_1 x_1)\,x_1,$$

so that he aims at x_1 given by

$$c - 2\,(k + l_1)\,x_1 - kx_2 - kD_{x_1}(x_2) = 0.$$

The second aims at x_2 given by

$$c - 2\,(k + l_2)\,x_2 - kx_1 - kD_{x_2}(x_1) = 0.$$

To solve these we should need to know x_2 as a function of x_1, and this depends on what each producer thinks the other is likely to do. There is then likely to be oscillation in the neighbourhood of the price given by the equation

marginal price for each = selling price,

unless they combine and arrange what each shall produce so as to maximize their combined profit.

§ 9. Alternative demand for factors; distribution of the factors of production among several commodities or among producers of different commodities.

The general problems of production of several commodities are discussed later, but without a complete analysis we can show how the proportions of the available factors are distributed when manufacturers of different products compete for their use.

Let $x_1 \dots x_r \dots x_m$ be quantities of m commodities produced, each by one manufacturer only, and μ_r be the cost of producing x_r.

Then $\mu_r = \pi_1 \cdot y_{r1} + \dots + \pi_s \cdot y_{rs} + \dots + \pi_\nu \cdot y_{r\nu}$,

where y_{rs} is the amount of Y_s used in producing x_r.

Then $D_{y_{rs}}(\mu_r) = \pi_s$, and similarly

$$\pi_s = D_{y_{1s}}(\mu_1) = \dots = D_{y_{rs}}(\mu_r) = \dots D_{y_{\nu s}}(\mu_m).$$

Hence any, the sth, factor is used till the marginal increment of the cost of the product due to the use of that factor is the same for all the commodities. If one person is producing two commodities he will have distributed his use of each factor till he gains nothing by diverting it from one undertaking to another.*

* See Marshall, *Principles of Economics*, Edn 1907, p. 848.

IV

SUPPLY OF AND DEMAND FOR THE FACTORS OF PRODUCTION

§ 1. Disutility. Labour.

So far it has been assumed that to any one manufacturer or producer, the prices of the factors $(\pi_1, \pi_2 ...)$ have been invariable and known.

We have now to determine equations relating to these factors, to obtain supply curves of the form $\pi'_s = \phi(y_s)$ and demand curves as $\pi_s = f(y_s)$, and to consider the equilibrium of supply and demand. We shall then, in a later chapter, bring together these new equations and those of demand for and supply of commodities.

The ultimate factors are labour, capital, and land as defined in economics. In production there are also intermediate factors such as raw materials and partly manufactured goods, whose prices are determinable from the general equations of the next chapter and need not be considered here.

Labour. Let $W(l)$ measure the disutility of labour, W involving a conception of the same character as U (utility), but of the opposite sign, so that $W(l)$ is negative.

The primitive theory was that a man worked till the fatigue, disagreeableness, or disutility of labour equalled at its margin the marginal utility of its reward or payment. Thus if he was producing Y which he intended to consume himself and y the amount produced was a function of l, the quantity of labour needed, he would maximize $U(y) + W(l)$, and stop when

$$\delta U(y) = -\delta W(l),$$
$$U_y . D_l(y) = -W_l,$$

when U_y is the marginal utility of y and W_l is the marginal disutility of labour.

Here $D_l(y)$ is the rate of production at the margin where he stops.

If A, instead of working for himself, is selling Y to B, who pays him in X, giving x units for y units, he stops when

$$\delta_1 U(x) = -\delta W(l),$$

$$\frac{\delta_1 U}{\delta x} \cdot \frac{\delta x}{\delta y} \cdot \frac{\delta y}{\delta l} = -\frac{\delta W}{\delta l}.$$

The ratio of $y : x$ equals the price, p, of X in terms of Y, $= \delta y : \delta x$ since it is the same for all units. Proceeding to the limit we have A's offer $\frac{1}{p} \cdot {}_1 U_x \cdot D_l(y) = -W_l,$

while B's offer is $x \cdot {}_2 U_x = y \cdot {}_2 U_y.$

If the production of y per unit time of labour is constant, or if instead of measuring labour by the hour we measure it by its output, $y = cl$, where c is a constant, and $D_l(y) = c$. By choice of units we may take $c = 1$ and A's offer becomes

$$x \cdot {}_1 U_x = -l \cdot W_l.$$

That is we simply write l for y, W_l for ${}_1 V_y$, and ${}_1 U_x$ for ${}_1 V_x$ in the equations of p. 8.

The above statement only holds good in modern industry in the relatively rare cases of production for one's self or directly for a consumer, or at will for an employer or a client.

It may be amended as follows:

Either, given the length of the working week, a quantity of labour or of Y is offered at any wage it will fetch.

Then y is known, and B's offer gives x in terms of y. $x/y = 1/p = p_2/p_1$ is the wage per unit y, $p_2 y$ is the cost of labour and equals $p_1 x$, the aggregate wage. Wages are in this case determined by the demand for the total of labour available.

Or, combined labour may fix the length of the working week by regard to average disutility of labour, the trade unions deciding at what point (having regard to the demand for labour) an hour's wage just compensates fatigue and loss of leisure for the ordinary man. In this case the original offer equations of A and of B apply, but A is a multiple person. This seems to be the best hypothesis for the sequel, the labour being divided into a number of groups (by locality and skill) with impassable barriers.

Also it is assumed that in equilibrium all available labour is employed, except when we consider labour as monopolized.

§ 2. Capital.

We do not need to know the nominal value of capital, but only the product which its use in conjunction with other factors gives in a year or other unit of time.

Let π'_c be the offer price for the use of capital giving a unit product, just as we took a price indifferently for labour or its product.

The nominal value of capital may be found either by its cost of replacement or by discounting its yield, problems which do not arise in the general equations of equilibrium.

Either, the amount of capital may be taken as fixed—A may have capital which is of no use to him, as a man may have labour ability which he cannot use to satisfy his own wants—in which case the demand curve will be sufficient to determine π'_c.

Or, there may be an offer curve for capital, in which case capital is simply the Y that A offers in the fundamental equations. A may either have physical capital (water power or a building) which he can use for his own direct purposes, or liquid capital which he can spend or invest, or transferable capital which he can lend to members of a society outside the group considered. This may be taken as the usual case, and in the sequel there are included disutility equations for capital.

Land. The classical theory of rent (apart from general theories of surplus value) depends on the consideration of the use of separate acres of land.* For the present purpose we may regard it as one

* See p. 70.

form of capital. If it is given in extent there is no disutility equation and there is one less unknown (y). But we obtain greater generality if we suppose that **A** owns land which he can either use for his own pleasure, or for production for himself, or lend to another for productive purposes.

§ 3. Equations of supply.

Thus for the three factors of production *either* the amount is known, *or* we have equations of the form

$$\frac{1}{\pi'_s} \cdot {}_tW_s = -\frac{1}{p_r} \cdot {}_tU_r = -{}_t\kappa,$$

where for the tth person ${}_tW_s$ is the marginal disutility of furnishing the factor Y_s, ${}_tU_r$ is the marginal utility of any commodity he receives in exchange, and in particular ${}_t\kappa$ is the marginal utility of money to him.

This gives the *supply equation* of a factor of production by a person (or multiple person) as

$$\pi'_s = -\frac{1}{{}_t\kappa} \cdot {}_tW_s = \phi(y_s).$$

§ 4. Equations of demand.

At present suppose the demand to be due to the use of a factor for the production of one commodity, X, regarded as typical of all. A more general method can easily be obtained by the reader after the next chapter.

We have

$$\mu = p'x = xf(x) = \pi_1 y_1 + \dots + \pi_s y_s + \dots + \pi_\nu y_\nu,$$

where $p = f(x)$ is the demand curve for x, and we take the case of no profit when $p' = p$, while $\dots\pi_s\dots$ is the price at which the factor $\dots Y_s\dots$ is bought.

Also we have the equations for the minimum cost of production (p. 29)

$$\frac{1}{\pi_1} \cdot F_{y_1} = \dots = \frac{1}{\pi_s} \cdot F_{y_s} = \dots = \frac{1}{\pi_\nu} \cdot F_{y_\nu}.$$

Omit μ, and eliminate all the y's except y_s. An equation is obtained involving y_s, $\pi_1 \ldots \pi_s \ldots \pi_\nu$, and p. Consider the variation of π_s and y_s only and write the *demand equation* as $\pi_s = f(y_s)$ where the function involves the supposed unvarying prices of the other commodities and of the commodity produced.

In competition $\pi'_s = \pi_s$, and therefore $f(y_s) = \phi(y_s)$ gives the position of equilibrium.

Combined labour or suppliers of any factor can maximize $y_s(\pi'_s - \pi_s)$, in which case

$$f(y_s) + y_s f'(y_s) = \phi(y_s) + y_s \phi'(y_s)$$

determines the value of y_s.

§ 5. The share of the factors.

We have $\pi_s = D_{y_s}(\mu)$.

Write $\eta_s = -\pi_s / y_s f'(y_s)$, the elasticity of the demand for Y_s.

If now y_s is increased by δy_s, the *amount* received by the suppliers of Y_s is increased by

$$D_{y_s}(\pi_s y_s) \cdot \delta y_s = (y_s D_{y_s}(\pi_s) + \pi_s) \delta y_s$$
$$= (y_s \cdot f'(y_s) + \pi_s) \cdot \delta y_s = \pi_s(1 - 1/\eta_s) \delta y_s.$$

This is positive, zero, or negative according as $\eta_s >$, $=$, or < 1.

If disutility is disregarded so that $\pi'_s = 0$, then in the case where $\eta_s < 1$, the amount received is greater if the supply is curtailed and reaches a maximum at

$$\eta_s = 1, \quad D_{y_s}(\pi_s y_s) = 0.$$

In this case, and in that of combination in § 4 where

$$D_{y_s}(\pi_s y_s) = D_{y_s}(\pi'_s y_s),$$

a trade union could increase the aggregate income and aggregate advantage of its members by raising their rate of wages and causing some to be out of work or to work short time. Every one, including those at play, could get more.

The *proportion* (ρ) of μ received increases by

$$D_{y_s}(\rho) \cdot \delta y_s = D_{y_s}(\pi_s y_s / \mu) \cdot \delta y_s = \left(\frac{\pi_s(1 - 1/\eta_s)}{\mu} - \frac{\pi_s^2 y_s}{\mu^2} \right) \cdot \delta y_s,$$

since $\pi_s = D_{y_s} \mu$, $\quad = \dfrac{\pi_s}{\mu}(1 - 1/\eta_s - \rho) \cdot \delta y_s.$

This is positive only if $\eta_s > 1/(1-\rho)$, and then is the greater the smaller is ρ.*

The *fall in price* paid per unit Y_s is

$$-\delta\pi_s = -f'(y_s) \cdot \delta y_s = \frac{\pi_s}{y_s\eta_s}\delta y_s.$$

* Pigou, *Economics of Welfare*, p. 710.

NOTATION.

n persons $A, B, C\ldots$, indicated by prefixes $1\ldots t\ldots n$.

m commodities $X_1\ldots X_r\ldots X_m$.

ν factors of production $Y_1\ldots Y_s\ldots Y_\nu$.

$x_1\ldots x_r\ldots x_m$ total quantities of $X_1\ldots$ consumed or saved, which equal total quantities produced.

$_t x_r$ quantity of X_r consumed or saved by t^{th} person.

$_t x'_r$ quantity of X_r produced by t^{th} person.

$y_1\ldots y_s\ldots y_\nu$ total quantities of $Y_1\ldots$ used, which equal total quantities supplied.

y_{rs} whole quantity of Y_s used in the manufacture of X_r.

$_t y_{rs}$ quantity by Y_s used by t^{th} person in the manufacture of X_r.

$_t y'_s$ quantity of Y_s supplied by t^{th} person.

F_r production function of X_r involving $y_1\ldots y_s\ldots y_\nu$.

$_t p'_r$ average cost of production of $_t x'_r$, i.e. cost per unit of production of X_r by t^{th} person.

p'_r supply price of X_r. $\quad p'_r = \phi_r(x_r)$. Supply function.

p_r demand price of X_r. $\quad p_r = f_r(x_r)$. Demand function.

π'_s supply price of Y_s. $\quad \pi'_s = \phi_s(y_s)$.

π_s demand price of Y_s. $\quad \pi_s = f_s(y_s)$.

$_t \kappa$ marginal utility of money to t^{th} person.

$_t U_r$ marginal utility of X_r to t^{th} person.

$_t W_s$ marginal disutility of supply of Y_s by t^{th} person.

$\mu_r = \chi_r(x_r)$, cost of producing x_r.

$\epsilon = \mu/x D_x \mu$.

$_t \mu$ expenditure of tth person in unit time.

$\eta = -f(x)/x f'(x) = $ elasticity of demand for a commodity.

$e = -\phi(x)/x \phi'(x) = $ elasticity of supply.

$\eta_s = -f_s(y_s)/y_s \cdot \phi_s(y_s) = $ elasticity of demand for Y_s.

$\psi(x) = f(x) - \phi(x) = p - p'$.

$m_t = {_t p'} \cdot x = $ cost of producing x by t^{th} person.*

$_t p'_m = $ marginal supply price of tth person in producing X, or average cost of production of X_m by t^{th} person, according to the context.

* Written μ on pp. 34–5.

V

GENERAL EQUATIONS OF SUPPLY AND DEMAND IN A STATIONARY POPULATION

§ 1. Interdependence of equations.

In the preceding chapters we have studied particular aspects of supply and demand under various hypotheses which limited the generality of the results; in order to reduce the unknowns to the number of conditions stated and to make the problems determinate it was necessary to assume that other quantities were for the time being invariable.

In fact the actual determination for any price or quantity involved depends on every other; we can only obtain a complete solution if we restrict our universe to two persons and two commodities, as in Chapter I, or extend it and include all conditions in any interdependent series of equations, as is done in the following paragraphs.

The notation of the previous chapters is followed, and their principal equations are introduced without further proof.

Let a community contain n persons who have no external commercial dealings (a restriction which can be modified without difficulty), who produce or manufacture and consume m commodities (such as X_r), whose supply depends on v factors of production (such as Y_s), the whole occurring in some fixed period, such as a year.

Let the tth person produce $_tx'_r$ of the rth commodity, and supply $_ty'_s$ of the sth factor, and let him consume or save $_tx_r$ of the rth commodity.

The equations allow for every person producing and using some of every commodity and factor, but it will easily be seen that when any of the quantities is zero a differential or other equation drops out.

§ 2. Supply equations.

Let x_r be the total amount of X_r produced, which is also the amount consumed or saved.

Let $\pi_1 \ldots \pi_s \ldots$ be the prices of factors per unit, taken as the same to all producers. If there is monopoly of any factor so that its supply price π' does not equal the price π paid for it, we should have sufficient additional equations of the form $\delta(\pi_1 - \pi'_1)y_1 = 0$ to allow the solution to be extended over the additional unknown.

Write y_s for the total amount of Y_s used by all persons for all purposes, y_{rs} the total used in the manufacture of X_r and $_t y_{rs}$ the amount used by the tth person in the manufacture of X_r. y_s is also the total amount of Y_s supplied.

Let $_t p'_r$ be the average cost per unit of X_r to the tth person in the manufacture of X_r.

We have the following equations:

Amounts produced

$$x_r = \sum_{t=1}^{t=n} {_t x'_r} \text{ for } r = 1, 2 \ldots m \qquad\qquad m \text{ equations.}$$

Production functions

$$_t x'_r = {_t F_r} ({_t y_{r1}} \ldots {_t y_{rs}} \ldots {_t y_{rv}}) \text{ for } \begin{array}{l} t = 1, 2 \ldots n \\ r = 1, 2 \ldots m \end{array} \qquad mn \text{ equations.}$$

Supply of factors

$$y_s = \sum_{t=1}^{t=n} {_t y'_s} \text{ for } s = 1, 2 \ldots v \qquad\qquad v \text{ equations.}$$

Whole use of factors

$$y_s = \sum_{r=1}^{r=m} y_{rs} \text{ for } s = 1, 2 \ldots v \qquad\qquad v \text{ equations.}$$

Use for separate commodities

$$y_{rs} = \sum_{t=1}^{t=n} {_t y_{rs}} \text{ for } \begin{array}{l} r = 1, 2 \ldots m \\ s = 1, 2 \ldots v \end{array} \qquad mv \text{ equations.}$$

Cost of production

$$_tp'_r \cdot {}_tx'_r = \sum_{s=1}^{s=\nu} \pi_s \cdot {}_ty_{rs} \quad \text{for} \quad \begin{matrix} t = 1, 2 \ldots n \\ r = 1, 2 \ldots m \end{matrix} \quad \middle| \quad mn \text{ equations.}$$

Law of substitution

$$\frac{1}{\pi_1} D_{y_1}({}_tF_r) = \ldots = \frac{1}{\pi_s} D_{y_s}({}_tF_r) = \ldots$$
$$= \frac{1}{\pi_\nu} D_{y_\nu}({}_tF_r) \quad \text{for} \quad \begin{matrix} t = 1, 2 \ldots n \\ r = 1, 2 \ldots m \end{matrix} \quad \middle| \quad mn\,(\nu - 1) \text{ equations.}$$

Disutility of supply of factors

$$\frac{1}{\pi_1} \cdot {}_tW_1 = \ldots = \frac{1}{\pi_s} \cdot {}_tW_s = \ldots = \frac{1}{\pi_\nu} \cdot {}_tW_\nu \quad \middle| \quad n\nu \text{ equations,}$$
$$= -{}_t\kappa \quad \text{for } t = 1, 2 \ldots n \quad \middle|$$

where $_t\kappa$ is the marginal utility of money to the tth person, not necessarily constant.

We have $mn\nu + mn + m\nu + n\nu + m + 2\nu$ equations for determining

$mn\nu$ *	quantities such as	$_ty_{rs}$
mn *	,, ,,	$_tx'_r$
mn	,, ,,	$_tp'_r$
$m\nu$ *	,, ,,	y_{rs}
$n\nu$ *	,, ,,	$_ty'_s$
m	,, ,,	x_r
ν *	,, ,,	y_s
ν *	,, ,,	π_s
n	,, ,,	$_t\kappa$

Eliminate those marked * and so obtain m supply equations † involving quantities such as x_r, $_tp'_r$, and $_t\kappa$.

If there is only one producer of each commodity and the costs per unit are $p'_1 \ldots p'_r \ldots p'_m$, or if there are several producers each with these costs, then we have p'_r instead of $_1p'_r$, $_2p'_r \ldots$ for each value of r, and m equations involving quantities such as x_r, p'_r, and $_t\kappa$.

[If during the exchange of X_r the variations in the quantities and prices of all other commodities and of the marginal utilities

† See Appendix, p. 94.

of money are negligible, these give simple supply equations $p'_r = \phi_r(x_r)$ as before, ϕ_r involving the unvarying quantities $x_1 \ldots x_{r-1},\ x_{r+1} \ldots x_m$, and $_1\kappa \ldots {}_n\kappa$.]

If there are many producers of X_r under decreasing return,† none on a scale to affect p'_r the joint offer price, the tth person adjusts $_t x'_r$ so as to maximize $(p'_r - {}_t p'_r) \cdot {}_t x'_r$, and we have

$$p'_r = {}_t p'_r + {}_t x_r \cdot D_{x_r}({}_t p'_r) \ddagger \ \text{ for } \ \begin{array}{l} t = 1 \ldots n \\ r = 1 \ldots m \end{array} \ \bigg| \ mn \text{ equations.}$$

If a person's limit is reached before the maximum, his $_t x_r$ is that of his greatest capacity.

These combined with the previous equations suffice to eliminate the mn terms $_t p'_r$, and we have in all cases m equations involving such quantities as $x_r,\ p'_r,\ {}_t\kappa$. (Result A.)

If a number of producers combine, they are to be treated as one producer whenever their combination affects the market.

§ 3. Demand equations.

Amounts consumed

$$x_r = \sum_{t=1}^{t=n} {}_i x_r \ \text{ for } \ r = 1, 2 \ldots m \ \bigg| \ m \text{ equations,}$$

where x_r, the total consumption, is the same as the total supply.

Utility equations

$$\frac{1}{p_1} \cdot {}_t U_1 = \ldots = \frac{1}{p_r} \cdot {}_t U_r = \ldots = \frac{1}{p_m} \cdot {}_t U_m = {}_t\kappa \ \bigg| \ mn \text{ equations.}$$
$$\text{for } t = 1, 2 \ldots n$$

Eliminate the mn quantities $_t x_r$ and so obtain m demand equations connecting quantities such as $p_r,\ x_r$, and $_t\kappa$. (Result B.)

[If during the exchange of the rth commodity variations in the prices and quantities of all other commodities and in the marginal utilities of money are negligible, this gives simple demand equations $p_r = f_r(x_r)$ as before, where f involves the unvarying quantities $x_1 \ldots x_{r-1},\ x_{r+1} \ldots x_m,\ {}_1\kappa \ldots {}_n\kappa$.]

---

† There can be only one producer in the long run under constant or increasing return, see pp. 36–7 above.

‡ The left-hand side of the equation $= {}_t p'_m$ the marginal supply price, p. 34.

§ 4. Combination of supply and demand equations.

We have from Results A and B $2m$ equations involving such quantities as x_r, p_r, p'_r, ${}_t\kappa$, or if ${}_t\kappa$ is eliminated $2m-n$ equations for $3m$ unknowns.

To complete the solution we have still to introduce two sets of relations, similar to those in Chapters II and III, pp. 21 and 37. The first takes into account the whole income of each person from the supply of factors or the net value of production, which must equal his expenditure together with saving. The second set connects p_1 with p'_1, p_2 with p'_2, &c. Thus for each person

$$\text{Income} = \text{expenditure} + \text{saving}.$$

Income from supply of factors is the sum of such terms as $\pi_s \cdot {}_t y'_s$, and that from production or manufacture of commodities the sum of such expressions as ${}_t x'_r \cdot (p_r - {}_t p'_r)$, the excess of selling over cost value.

Hence for the tth person

$$\sum_{s=1}^{s=\nu} \pi_s \cdot {}_t y'_s + \sum_{r=1}^{r=m} (p_r - {}_t p'_r) \cdot {}_t x'_r = \sum_{r=1}^{r=m} p_r \cdot {}_t x_r \qquad n \text{ equations.}$$
$$\text{for } t = 1, 2 \ldots n$$

But the total of the left-hand expressions equals (from the cost of production equations) the total of the right-hand expressions, when all incomes are added together, and therefore the group gives only $n-1$ new equations.

Now combining all the equations, and eliminating n such terms at ${}_t\kappa$, we have $2m-1$ equations connecting the $3m$ quantities such as x_r, p_r, p'_r, all other quantities being eliminated.

To connect p_r with p'_r we must distinguish between competition and monopoly.

When the exchanges take place under competition

$$p_r = p'_r,$$

or when there is producers' monopoly *

$$\delta (p_r - p'_r) x_r = 0 \text{ for } r = 1, 2 \ldots m,$$

where p_r and p'_r involve x_r.

m equations.

* For consumers' combination, see p. 64 below.

Eliminate p'_r and we have $2m-1$ equations, sufficient to determine $x_1...x_m$ and the price-ratios $p_1 : p_2 : ... : p_m$.

If the mth commodity is money, $p_m = 1$ and all prices are determinate. If money is solely precious metal produced and circulated commercially, x'_m (the amount of it produced) is obtained from the equations. If the supply of money is gerrymandered, so that the tth person obtains m_t units of currency for nothing, m_t would be added to his income ; but analysis is not capable of dealing with undefined political interference with currency. If, however, the aggregate income as in a socialist state were given and the method of its distribution, the equations might become determinate.

The above analysis has proceeded by successive elimination, but it is evident that there are sufficient equations to determine every x, y, p, π, &c., involved. Further, a change in any one of the multitudinous equations affects the solution for every quantity and price ; the whole is interdependent, and it is only by arbitrarily assuming constancy where none exists that isolated examination is possible. We can, however, with due caution assume that when one quantity varies some consequent variations have negligible effects ; and we can also after eliminating a group of quantities study interactions in the remaining group.

In the groups of equations those which express mere identities should be distinguished from those which depend on volition, and the hypotheses relating to the latter should be specially studied. They may perhaps be classified as industrial, commercial, or hedonistic.

Industrial: the law of substitution involving

$$\frac{1}{\pi_s} \cdot D_s \left({}_t F_r \right).$$

Commercial: the maximizing of

$$(p'_r - {}_t p'_r) \cdot {}_t x'_r, \ (p'_r - p_r) \, x_r, \ (\pi_1 - \pi'_1) y_1,$$

where some absence of competition allows it.

Hedonistic: $$\frac{1}{\pi_s} \cdot {}_t W_s = -{}_t \kappa = \frac{1}{p_r} \cdot {}_t U_r.$$

It is only this last group that is seriously open to criticism. It depends ultimately on the idea discussed in the opening pages (1–3), and it should be noticed that it does not involve the third postulate.

There remains the general assumption that persons in economic matters act under economic motives with adequate knowledge. There are many transfers of wealth on other grounds, and the equations are not always pressed to the maximum. Also ignorance and miscalculation are common, and the mere clinging to custom may prevent advantageous changes.

§ 5. Stability of equilibrium.

The whole solution is statical. If exchanges were established at the rates given by the equations, no forces would disturb them till some of the constants involved (such as the number of persons) changed. The questions at once arise whether there is more than one set of solutions and whether the equilibrium is stable.

There is nothing in the nature of the case to prevent multiple solutions, but in practice if we had any numerical values there is not likely to be difficulty in knowing which set is appropriate. Whether the position is stable can be judged from the intersection of the pairs of demand and supply curves for each factor and commodity as discussed in the following chapter. There is stability if the supply curve crosses the demand curve from below on the left to above on the right. If an unstable position were momentarily obtained, there would be adjustment till the next position of stable equilibrium was reached.

Though the solution is statical it is generally possible (as in most statical problems) to determine in what direction the system will move if there is a given change in any of the constants, as for example more land, capital, materials, or labourers brought into the system. But an actual solution, when defined changes take place continually over a period, would involve complicated analysis, and little progress has as yet been made in such an investigation.

It should be added that in the preceding analysis the X's and Y's have been kept distinct artificially. In fact, the results of one production may enter as materials in another, so that an X_r may be a Y_s. There is no serious analytical difficulty in allowing for this and obtaining the requisite number of equations, but the treatment would become more complicated and would not lead to compensating enlightenment. The marginal utility of equations has probably been reached.

In the following chapter certain problems arising out of these equations are discussed.

VI

APPLICATIONS OF THE GENERAL EQUATIONS

§ 1. The inclination of the demand curve.

As a preliminary we will discuss the direction of a demand curve.

Our equations for one consumer are

$$\mu = p_1 x_1 + \dots + p_r x_r + \dots + p_m x_m,$$

$$\frac{1}{p_1} \cdot U_1 = \dots = \frac{1}{p_r} \cdot U_r = \dots = \frac{1}{p_m} \cdot U_m = \kappa,$$

where $x_1 \dots x_m$ are bought in a unit of time during which his whole expenditure is μ, and his marginal utility of money is κ.

If the uses of $X_1, X_2 \dots$ are *independent*, U_1 does not involve any x except x_1, and therefore $U_{12}* = D_{x_2}(U_1)$ is zero, and similarly $U_{r, r'} = 0$ for all pairs r, r'.

In this case $p_1 = \frac{1}{\kappa} \cdot U_1$ is the demand curve, and if κ is not sensibly affected by the amount of dealings in X_1, $D_{x_1} p_1 = \frac{1}{\kappa} \cdot U_{11}$, which is negative if utility grows by diminishing increments when x_1 increases by equal increments, an assumption discussed on p. 13 above.

If the uses are not independent, we have (κ still constant)

$$\kappa D_x p_1 = U_{11} + U_{12} \cdot D_{x_1}(x_2) + \dots, \quad \text{(see Formula 7, p. 88)}$$

and the sign is indeterminate till we have further information. There may be cases where U_{12} and $D_{x_1}(x_2)$ have the same sign and their product is greater than $-U_{11}$.

Consider two commodities only, and let μ and p_2 be kept constant while $p_1, x_1,$ and x_2 change. In such a case κ is not constant.

---

* U_1 stands for $D_{x_1}(U)$, $x_2 \dots$const., and U_{12} for $D_{x_2}(U_1)$, $x_1, x_3 \dots$const.

The equations are $\quad p_1 x_1 + p_2 x_2 = \mu,$
$$p_2 \cdot U_1 - p_1 \cdot U_2 = 0,$$
which will give the demand curve for x_1, if x_2 is eliminated.

To examine these, take the utility surface in the form
$$U = -a x_1^2 - 2 h x_1 x_2 - b x_2^2 + 2 g x_1 + 2 f x_2,$$
so that $\qquad U_1 = -2(a x_1 + h x_2 - g),$
$$U_2 = -2(h x_1 + b x_2 - f),$$
$$U_{11} = -2a, \quad U_{12} = -2h, \quad U_{22} = -2b.$$

a and b are then positive.

Then $\qquad p_2(a x_1 + h x_2 - g) - p_1(h x_1 + b x_2 - f) = 0,$
and, x_2 being eliminated, the demand equation for x_1 is
$$b p_1^2 \cdot x_1 - 2 h p_2 \cdot p_2 x_1 - (\mu b - p_2 f) p_1 + a p_2^2 \cdot x_1 + \mu h p_2 - p_2^2 g = 0,$$
where p_1 and x_1 are the only variables.

Then
$$D_{x_1} p_1 \cdot (2 b p_1 x_1 - 2 h p_2 x_1 + p_2 f - \mu b) = -b p_1^2 + 2 h p_2 p_1 - a p_2^2,$$
which can be expressed as
$$D_x p_1 \cdot (b p_1 x_1 - h p_2 x_1 + \tfrac{1}{2} p_2 U_2) = -b p_1^2 + 2 h p_2 p_1 - a p_2^2,$$
where a, b, and U_2 are positive.

If h is zero or negative, i. e. U_{12} zero or positive, and the uses of X_1 and X_2 independent or complementary, then $D_x p_1$ is negative.

§ 2. The case of alternative demand.

If h is positive, i. e. the uses of X_1 and X_2 alternative, then $D_x p_1$ may be positive or negative.

A case is found in which $D_x p_1$ is positive, when the utility surface is $\qquad z = -x_1 x_2 + 40 x_1 + 100 x_2,$
and the income equation is
$$p_1 x_1 + p_2 x_2 = 840,$$
and p_2 is fixed at 40.

Then $U_1 = 40 - x_2$, $U_2 = 100 - x_1$, and the demand curve is found to be $\qquad p_1 x_1 - 50 p_1 + 380 = 0.$
$$\therefore \; D_{x_1}(p_1) = \frac{p_1}{50 - x_1},$$
which is positive when $x_1 < 50$.

If at one time $p_1 = 10$, then $x_1 = 12$, $x_2 = 18$. Now let p_1 rise to 12; then $x_1 = 18\frac{1}{3}$, $x_2 = 15\frac{1}{2}$ satisfy the equations. That is, a rise in the price of X_1 causes a greater consumption of X_1 and a smaller consumption of X_2 in these particular conditions.

Similarly, if the price of X_1 were fixed, we should have

$$D_{x_2}(p_2) = \frac{p_2}{20 - x_2},$$

and, if p_2 rose, x_2 would increase if it started at less than 20.

Mr. W. E. Johnson deals with this problem more exactly in the *Economic Journal*, 1913, pp. 500 seq.—pages which suggested the paragraph above.

As the double result is surprising it is worth while to show that it can be illustrated.

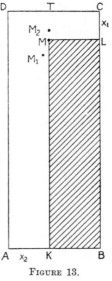

A purchaser wishes to spend £840 on land for a house and garden; he wants at least 15 yards frontage, and apart from that he aims at maximizing the area. A rectangular plot has frontage 40 yards (AB), and depth 100 yards (AD). A purchaser buying frontage AK (x_2) obtains the land $AKTD$, and may buy an addition in the strip $TCBK$ at £p_1 a yard measured from C; he can only buy up to say half this strip. Let him buy CL (x_1). The portion not bought is shaded.

The area bought is

FIGURE 13.

$$40 \times 100 - (40 - x_2)(100 - x_1),$$

and the amount spent is $p_1 x_1 + p_2 x_2 = 840$. Hence we have the equations just given.

At $p_2 = 40$, $p_1 = 10$, the corner point M is at $x_1 = 12$, $x_2 = 18$.

At $p_2 = 40$, $p_1 = 12$, M_1 is at $x_1 = 18\frac{1}{3}$, $x_2 = 15\frac{1}{2}$; thus x_1 is increased; but at $p_2 = 42$, $p_1 = 10$, M_2 is at $x_1 = 8$, $x_2 = 18\cdot1$, and x_2 is increased.

§ 3. Demand for and supply of one commodity : competition and monopoly.

We now return to the subject of Chapter II, no longer considering exchange between possessors of goods as there, but separating producers from consumers.

If $_t\mu$ is the tth consumer's expenditure in the unit of time, and the other letters have the same meaning as in Chapter V,

$$_t\mu = \sum_{r=1}^{r=m} p_r \cdot {}_t x_r, \text{ for } t = 1, 2 \ldots n \qquad \qquad n \text{ equations.}$$

$$x_r = \sum_{t=1}^{t=n} {}_t x_r, \text{ for } r = 1, 2 \ldots m \qquad \qquad m \text{ equations.}$$

$$\frac{1}{p_1} \cdot {}_t U_{x_1} = \ldots = \frac{1}{p_r} \cdot {}_t U_r = \ldots = \frac{1}{p_m} {}_t U_m, \qquad n(m-1) \text{ equations.}$$
$$\text{for } t = 1, 2 \ldots n$$

Eliminate the mn quantities $_t x_r$ and we have m equations connecting such quantities as p_r with such quantities as x_r and $_t\mu$. Suppose the μ's given. Solve these equations separately for the p's and we have demand equations

$$p_r = f_r (x_1 \ldots x_r \ldots x_m).$$

Similarly from pp. 49, 50, if we take the marginal utilities of money to the producers as constant, we have supply equations

$$p_r' = \phi_r (x_1 \ldots x_r \ldots x_m).$$

Though all the x's are involved in each equation, we may study their variation independently. Supposing then all the quantities except those of X_1 to remain unchanged, we have for X_1

$$p = f(x), \quad p' = \phi(x).$$

Ignore such exceptional cases as those treated in the last paragraph and take $f'(x)$ to be negative.

$\phi'(x)$ is positive, zero, or negative according as the return is decreasing, constant, or increasing in the sense of Chapter III.

Pure competition. Here we suppose that no producer can affect the price, and that the entrepreneur's earnings are included under one of the factors of production.

In this case $p = p'$, $f(x) = \phi(x)$ gives the solution. The position is stable when at it the supply curve crosses from below the demand curve on the left as in the figures.

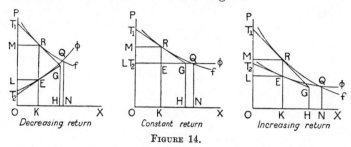

Decreasing return   Constant return   Increasing return

FIGURE 14.

For if the price NQ at the quantity ON gives the intersection of the curves, then if less than ON is produced the demand price is higher than the supply price and production is increased, while if more than ON is produced the excess cannot be sold at so much as it cost and production is diminished.

Monopoly. Suppose that there is only one producer * and that the consumers have no alternative for the commodity and are not combined.

If the monopolist aims solely at maximizing his profit, he will fix x so as to make $(p - p') x$ a maximum, where p' is his average cost price when he is producing x in the unit of time.

Then if a production x_1 gives the maximum, x_1 satisfies

$$D_x \{ (f(x) - \phi(x)) x \} = 0.$$

Write $\psi(x)$ for $f(x) - \phi(x)$. Then

$$\psi(x_1) + x_1 \psi'(x_1) = 0.$$

In the figures

$$OK = x_1, \quad KR = f(x_1), \quad KE = \phi(x_1), \quad ER = \psi(x_1).$$

$x_1 . \phi'(x_1) = T_2 L$, positive in (i), zero in (ii), negative in (iii); $x_1 . f'(x_1) = -MT_1$, where $T_1 R$, $T_2 E$ are tangents to the curves, and OK is the quantity at the maximum profit,

$$ER = \psi(x_1) = -x_1 . \psi'(x_1) = T_2 L + MT_1,$$

and therefore $ER = \frac{1}{2} T_1 T_2$, in all cases.

* The profits of individual producers in competition, and of two producers in duopoly, are discussed in Chapter III above. The former case is also included in the general equations. Here one important case is discussed in more detail.

In competition the quantity would be ON, and the price would be NQ if the curves meet at Q, *if monopolizing did not alter the supply curve.*

Let the tangents meet at G and draw GH perpendicular to OX; then $OK = \frac{1}{2}OH$.

Consider the relative positions of H and N. If in the regions RQ, EQ the curves are approximately straight, G and Q and therefore H and N nearly coincide, and supply under pure monopoly is approximately half that under pure competition. The increase in price is of course in all cases $f(x_1) - f(ON)$; this equals $\dfrac{NQ}{2\eta}$ where η is the elasticity of demand at Q, if the tangent at Q is a sufficient approximation to the curve QR. The rise is the greater the less the elasticity.

In fact, however, the increase in price made by the monopolist is influenced by certain considerations.

The process of monopolizing may introduce considerable reductions in cost of production, but the supply curve would have to be lowered very greatly (in the case of constant return approximately by LT_1) to bring R back to Q.

If the price is high there is an inducement to use substitutes, and the public may tend to give up the use of the commodity.

If profits are great, there is an inducement for rivals to try to break the monopoly.

If in deference to public opinion the monopolist lowers the price he may make a small sacrifice in his profits and increase the output perceptibly (see p. 25). If η is elasticity of demand, the quantity will be increased from x_1 to $x_1(1 + \lambda)$, if the price is lowered from p to $p\left(1 - \dfrac{\lambda}{\eta}\right)$, while the profits fall only from P to $P(1 - \lambda^2)$, approximately.

If the monopolist makes no economies and exercises his power to the full, it will be seen from the figures that in ordinary cases of constant and of increasing return OK is less than $\frac{1}{2}ON$, while in decreasing return it may be greater or less.

§ 4. Various questions of monopoly and combination.

I. There is nothing to prevent monopoly in the *production of all commodities*, if the factors of production are not also monopolized.

If in the general equations X_m is money and therefore $p_m = 1$ and there is only one producer of each commodity, we have (as on pp. 49, 50) sufficient equations to obtain

$$p_r = f_r(x_1...x_r...x_m),\ p'_r = \phi_r(x_1...x_r...x_m)$$

for each commodity, and the monopolists' equations

$$\delta(p_r - p'_r)x_r$$

are not inconsistent with each other.

II. If production is not, but the *factors of production* are, monopolized, so that the first person controls Y_1, the second Y_2, and so on:

In the case of the first factor $_2y'_1$, $_3y'_1...{_n}y'_1$ are zero, the equations $\frac{1}{\pi_2} \cdot {_t}W_2 =$, $\frac{1}{\pi_3} \cdot {_t}W_3 =$, &c. drop out, and the supplier aims at maximizing $(\pi_1 - \pi'_1)y_1$, so that

$$\delta\{(\pi_1 - \pi'_1)y_1\} = 0.$$

For example, take the case of one commodity X_1, two factors Y_1, Y_2 (say labour and capital), and one multiple purchaser with prefix 3.

The demand curve for X_1 is $\frac{1}{p_1} \cdot {_3}U_1 = {_3}\kappa$, say $p_1 = f(x_1)$.

The producer's equation is $x_1 = F(y_1 y_2)$, where

$$\frac{1}{\pi_1}F_{y_1} = \frac{1}{\pi_2} \cdot F_{y_2},$$

and, *if the producer makes no profit*,

$$p_1 x_1 = \pi_1 y_1 + \pi_2 y_2.$$

Eliminating p_1 and x_1, we can obtain separately π_1 and π_2 as functions of y_1 and y_2.

Let the supply equations of the factors be

$$\pi'_1 = \phi_1(y_1)\ \text{and}\ \pi'_2 = \phi_2(y_2).$$

Then if y_1 and y_2 are independent of each other, the monopolist equations

$$D_{y_1}\{(\pi_1 - \pi'_1)y_1\} = 0\ \text{and}\ D_{y_2}\{(\pi_2 - \pi_2')y_2\} = 0$$

are capable of solution and give determinate results.

Similarly all the factors can be monopolized with determinate results.

III. *Bilateral monopoly.* If, however, the *producer is also monopolist* and makes a profit, the case is different.

For simplicity take only one factor.

Our equations are

$$p_1 = f(x_1), \quad x_1 = F(y_1), \quad p'_1 x_1 = \pi_1 y_1, \quad \pi'_1 = \phi(y_1).$$

Take $F(y_1) = y_1$ for further simplicity. Then

$$p'_1 = \pi_1, \quad p_1 = f(x_1), \quad \pi'_1 = \phi(x_1)$$

are the only equations.

Manufacturer tries to maximize $\{f(x_1) - \pi_1\} x_1$.

Labourer „ „ $\{\pi_1 - \phi(x_1)\} x_1$.

The manufacturer fixes in a particular π_1 and produces x'_1 to make his maximum. At the same π_1 the labourer furnishes x''_1. There may be a value of π_1 for which $x'_1 = x''_1$, but without collusion it will not be obtained.

This result, that with one factor and one user of that factor the equations become indeterminate, is obtainable with less simple hypotheses; but the method used can be extended to show that universal monopoly of all factors and all production leads to indeterminate results.

IV. *Consumer's combination.* The next question to examine is whether purchasers of goods can obtain any advantage by acting together instead of competing, and what special power is in the hands of a person who is the sole purchaser of some special commodity.

Let $p' = \phi(x)$ be the supply price of X.

If a purchaser cannot influence p' his gain in utility by purchasing x units is a maximum at that position on his own offer curve where $U_x = \kappa p'$. (Point Q, Figure 5, p. 23.)

If, however, he can influence price he can aim at that point on the seller's offer curve, where it reaches highest up the purchaser's utility surface. (Point Q_2, Figure 1, p. 6.) It can readily be shown that at this position $U_x = \kappa D_x \{x\phi(x)\}$,* from the consideration that one tangent at Q_2 touches both curves, and therefore $U_x = \kappa\phi(x) + \kappa x\phi'(x)$.†

[Otherwise, his gain in utility is $U(x) - \kappa x\phi(x)$, that is the advantage of receiving x less the utility of the money he pays.

* Offer curve $y = x\phi(x)$, gradient of utility surface U_x/κ.

† See *Economics of Welfare*, p. 283.

If κ is taken as constant, this is a maximum when $U_x = \kappa p'$, if p' is constant, and when $U_x = \kappa p' + \kappa x D_x p'$ when p' varies.]

Write $p = \frac{1}{\kappa} U_x = f(x)$, for the equation of the purchaser's demand.

In the case of decreasing return $\phi'(x)$ is positive, of increasing return it is negative.

If Q is the intersection of the demand and supply curves, the quantity ON will be sold at the price NQ, if the purchaser cannot influence price.

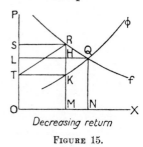

Decreasing return

FIGURE 15.

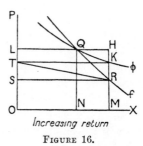

Increasing return

FIGURE 16.

If he can influence price he will get the greatest advantage at a quantity OM and a price MK, when MK produced meets the demand curve at a point R, such that if KT parallel to XO meets OP at T, TR is parallel to the tangent at K; for then

$$x \cdot \phi'(x) = KR = MR - MK = f(x) - \phi(x) = \frac{1}{\kappa} U_x - \phi(x),$$

the condition required.

By reference to p. 34 it will be seen MK is the seller's marginal supply price at M. The proposition may then be stated thus : under competition the purchaser pays the seller's supply price, while if the purchaser is only one (or several combined) while there are competitive sellers, he can pay the seller's marginal supply price.

While in diminishing return purchases are restricted and the price lowered, under increasing return the lowering of price and the maximizing of purchaser's advantage is obtained by extending the purchases.

In both figures draw QL and RS parallel to XO to meet OP, and let QL meet RK in H.

In decreasing return the loss of utility from the decreased possession of X is

$$U(ON) - U(OM) = \int_{OM}^{ON} U_x \cdot dx = MNQR.$$

The gain by decreased expenditure is the gnomon $TLQNMK$. Excess of gain is $LTKH - QHR$.

In increasing return the gain of utility by possession is $QNMR$, the loss by increased expenditure $TKMO - LQNO$, and the excess of gain is $LTKH - QHR$ as before.

The general position when either buying or selling may be competitive or not may be further elucidated as follows.

If there are two persons, A buying and B selling X, and A paying and B receiving Y (money), then A's offer is $_1U_x - p \cdot _1\kappa = 0$, and B's offer is $_2U_x - p' \cdot _2\kappa = 0$.

If B raises his price above p', he makes extra profit, and some one else will presumably undersell him. But if he has monopoly he aims at $\delta(p - p')x = 0$.

A may, however, refuse to buy at the higher price, and both are satisfied only at $p = p'$, $_2\kappa \cdot _1U_x = _1\kappa \cdot _2U_x$.

If there are several buyers not in collusion and B is the only seller, B can fix price.

If there are several sellers not in collusion and one buyer A, A can choose p' so as to maximize his net gain in utility, which will give the position illustrated by the figures above.

Since the analysis of consumers' combinations is not so familiar as that of seller's monopoly, a numerical illustration may be studied with advantage.

Let the supply equation be $p' = \phi(x) = 30 - 2x$, and let the purchaser's utility be $U(x) = 42x - 3x^2$, so that the demand equation is $p = U_x = 42 - 6x = f(x)$, $_1\kappa$ being taken as unity.

Then the purchaser's net advantage is maximized when

$$U(x) - x\phi(x) = 12x - x^2 = 36 - (x - 6)^2$$

is greatest; that is when $x = 6$, $p' = 18$.

The competitive price on the other hand would be where $f(x) = \phi(x)$, $x = 3$, $p' = 24$.

x	$U(x)$	U_x	$\phi(x)$	$x\phi(x)$	$U(x) - x\phi(x)$
2	72	30	26	52	20
3	99	24	24	72	27
4	120	18	22	88	32
5	135	12	20	100	35
6	144	6	18	108	36
7	147	0	16	112	35

Now if the demand was made up by two identical demands, viz.: $f(x_1) = 42 - 12x_1$, each for x_1 half the former quantity, then if they competed they would each spend 36d. on $1\frac{1}{2}$ articles, at 24d. each; if they combined they could each get 3 for 54d., at 18d. each. The net utility for each is $42x_1 - 6x_1^2 - p'.x_1$, which is $13\frac{1}{2}$ when $x_1 = 1\frac{1}{2}$ and $p' = 24$, but 18 when $x_1 = 3$ and $p' = 18$.

This is a case where two people by combining are able to take advantage of increasing return in supply.

In decreasing return the advantage is obtained by restricting purchases. Thus if we write $\phi(x) = 30 + 2x$, $U(x)$ being as before, in competition each person buys $\frac{3}{4}$ at $p' = 33$, and his net utility is $3\frac{3}{8}$; in combination each person buys $\frac{3}{5}$ at $p' = 32\frac{2}{5}$, and his net utility is 3·6.

This is a case where two people avoid the expense of increasing the supply.

§ 5. Joint and composite demand and supply.

In the general equations there was no assumption that the demand or supply of the commodities or factors were independent of each other, and in the first section of this chapter special cases of dependence were considered. But it will be useful to show how the various problems considered in Marshall's *Principles of Economics*, bk. v, chap. vi (in the text, notes, and corresponding Appendix), are related to the system.

The X's are 'consumers' goods', 'of the first order', 'in direct demand'. The Y's are 'producers' goods and factors', 'of the second order', 'in indirect demand'.

The quantities $y_{r1}...y_{rs}...y_{rv}$ (see p. 48) are *jointly demanded* for the production of x_r, as for example labour, coal, ore, transport, pig-iron.

The quantities $y_{1s}...y_{rs}...y_{ms}$ are under a *composite* or *alternative demand* for use in various manufactures : e.g. Y_s may be labour.

The necessary equations for these two cases have already been given.

Composite or *alternative supply* occurs when a want can be supplied by X_r or X_{r+1} (e. g. by beef or by mutton). Choose units (e.g. weight of beef and of mutton) so that $p_r = p_{r+1}$. Let the relation be so close that they are perfect alternatives, so that $_tx_r + _tx_{r+1} = _tx_r{}'$ (say) cannot be separated into its terms. There is nothing to decide the preference of the consumer.

Then in the utility equations (p. 50)

$$= \frac{1}{p_r} \cdot {}_tU_r = \frac{1}{p_{r+1}} \cdot {}_tU_{r+1} =$$

is replaced by
$$= \frac{1}{p_r} D_{x_{r'}} ({}_tU_{r'}) =$$

for each of n persons, and n equations are lost and n fewer quantities determined.

Equations $x_r = \sum_{t=1}^{t=n} {}_tx_r$ and $x_{r+1} = \sum_{t=1}^{t=n} {}_tx_{r+1}$

are replaced by
$$x'_{r'} = \sum_{t=1}^{t=n} {}_tx'_{r'},$$

while the lost equation is made good by $p_r = p_{r+1}$.

In the expenditure equations $+ p_r \cdot {}_tx_r + p_{r+1} \cdot {}_tx_{r+1} +$ is replaced by $+ p_r \cdot {}_tx_r{}' +$.

The remaining equations are unaltered. The amounts produced of X_r and X_{r+1} are determinate, and the totals of the two consumed by each person.

Joint supply occurs when X_r and X_{r+1} are produced by the same process in a determinate proportion (e.g. gas and coke). If l_t is the proportion for the tth producer, the equation for the production function $_tx'_{r+1} = {}_tF_{r+1}$ is replaced by $_tx'_{r+1} = l_t \cdot {}_tx'_r$.

The equations involving the suffix $\overline{r+1}$ drop out in the cost of production, separate use of factors, and substitution of factors. In all $n+v+n\,(v-1) = v\,(n+1)$ equations drop out. At the same time the $v\,(n+1)$ quantities

$$y_{r+1,\,s}, \;\; _1y_{r+1,\,s}, \;\; _2y_{r+1,\,s}, \cdots n y_{r+1,\,s} \;\; \text{for } s = 1,\,2\ldots v$$

cease to exist.

If we regard X_{r+1} as the by-product, then instead of

$$\delta\,({p'}_{r+1} - {}_t{p'}_{r+1})\,x_{r+1} = 0, \;\; \text{we have } {}_t{p'}_{r+1} = 0.$$

The demand equations are unaltered and the solution is completely determinate.

[More simply, if we consider the supply and demand of X_r and X_{r+1}, ignoring all other changes and assuming no profit, and taking only one producer, then

$$x_{r+1} = lx_r,$$

$$p_r x_r + p_{r+1} x_{r+1} = x_r \cdot \phi\,(x_r),$$

and

$$\frac{1}{p_r} U_r = \frac{1}{p_{r+1}} U_{r+1} = \kappa,$$

where $\phi\,(x_r)$ is the cost of producing x_r and x_{r+1} combined, give sufficient equations.]

The *commodities* X_r and X_{r+1} are *jointly demanded*, if each is only useful with the other (e.g. pens and ink).

Take the units so that one unit of X_r is wanted with one of X_{r+1}. Then we have n new equations

$$_t x_r = {}_t x_{r+1} \;\; \text{for } t = 1,\,2\ldots n,$$

while in the utility equations

$$= \frac{1}{p_r} \cdot {}_t U_r = \frac{1}{p_{r+1}} \cdot {}_t U_{r+1} =$$

are replaced by

$$= \frac{1}{p_r + p_{r+1}} \cdot {}_t U_{r'},$$

where $_t U_{r'}$ is the marginal utility of a unit of X_r and X_{r+1} together, so that these n equations are lost.

The remaining equations are unaffected, so that the solution is uniquely determinate.

The *Derived* or *indirect demand* for factors of production may be studied from the following point of view. For simplicity consider one commodity X; suppose its demand equation to be $p = f(x)$, and that its production depends on the factors $Y_1 \ldots Y_\nu$. Required to determine the demand for Y_1, that is the prices that will be paid for various amounts of Y_1, when the prices of the remaining factors (which of course are jointly demanded with it) are constant.

We have then the equations :

$$p = p', \text{ if there is no profit,}$$

$$x = F(y_1, y_2 \ldots),$$

$$p = f(x),$$

$$p'x = \pi_1 y_1 + \ldots + \pi_s y_s + \ldots + \pi_\nu y_\nu,$$

and
$$\frac{1}{\pi_1} . F_{y_1} = \ldots = \frac{1}{\pi_s} F_{y_s} = \ldots = \frac{1}{\pi_\nu} F_{y_\nu},$$

from which we can eliminate the quantities $y_2 \ldots y_\nu$, p, p' and x and so obtain an equation between π_1 and y_1, involving the constants of the functions and the unvarying prices $\pi_2, \pi_3 \ldots \pi_\nu$.

VII

SURPLUS VALUE, RENT, AND TAXATION

§ 1. Producers' surplus.

A surplus is obtained when a producer sells for more than his cost price or a consumer buys for less than he is willing to give.

Thus the various producers of X_r are not assumed in the previous sections to incur the same cost price. The differences are due either to situation or to skill of management or to other special circumstances ; the first gives rise to rent, the second to personal surplus.

It is perhaps simplest to assume that part of the entrepreneur's receipts are due to his own labour, included in one of the Y's, and then the marginal producer gets wages of management and no profits.

If all producers are equally favourably situated, then under constant or under increasing return the most skilled tends to get all the trade, till and unless its magnitude becomes too great for his ability.

Under decreasing return many producers may remain in the industry, and we have the position described above (p. 50) of which the extreme case is when no producer supplies enough to affect the price significantly. Then the tth person maximizes $(p_r - {}_tp_r) \cdot {}_tx'_r$, so that

$$D_{x_r}({}_tp_r \cdot x'_r) = p_r.$$

Write (cf. p. 34) $m_t = {}_tp' \cdot x$, suppressing the r's.

The tth producer's profit is

$${}_tx' \cdot D_x(m_t) - m_t = {}_tx' \cdot {}_tp'_m - m_t,$$

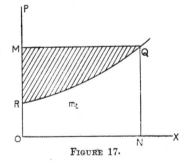

FIGURE 17.

where ${}_tp'_m = D_x(m_t)$ is his marginal supply price, NQ, while ${}_tx' = ON$, and RQ is his marginal supply curve.

Then $\quad m_t = \int_0^{t^{x'}} D_x(m_t) \cdot dx = \int_0^{t^{x'}} {}_t p'_m \cdot dx = $ area $ORQN,$*

and ${}_t x' \cdot {}_t p'_m = $ area $MQRN$, where QM is parallel to XO.

The profit is the shaded portion QRM (Figure 17).

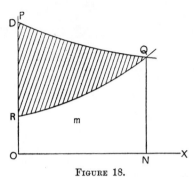

FIGURE 18.

Now take the case of only one producer (Figure 18).

Let $p = f(x)$ be the demand curve ; p is not now given.

Write $p_m = D_x(px) = D_x(xf(x)) = NQ$, and in the figure let DQ be the locus of Q. This curve differs both from the usual demand curve $p = f(x)$ and from the offer curve $y = xf'(x)$.

The producer modifies p' and therefore x so as to maximize $(p-p')x$, i.e. $px - m$, so that at equilibrium

$$D_x(m) = D_x(px),$$

and therefore $p'_m = p_m = NQ$.

Then $\quad px = \int_0^x p_m dx * = $ area $ODQN$, while $m = $ area $ORQN$ as before.

The profit is

area $ODQN - $ area $ORQN = $ area DRQ,

which is greater than before, if (as is usual) $D_x(p_m)$ is negative.

§ 2. Economic rent.

Land has so far entered into the equations only as a factor of production measured not in superficies, but by units of produce.

---

* See Appendix, pp. 92 seq. In each figure Q is marked at the position of equilibrium. ${}_t p'_m$, p_m and x are variables in the integrations, but have their definite values ON, NQ in the statements of equilibrium.

Special theorems of rent depend partly on the different productivity of different acres, varying also according to their cultivation, partly on the assumption that the whole area cannot be increased.

In fact we do not deal in this book with the influence of prices on new supplies of labour and capital, except in so far as labourers may be drawn from working for themselves or idling, and capital from use by its owner or non-use. Similarly we have assumed that land is limited, and either is all used for production for exchange or can be used by its owner for his own enjoyment.

Suppose a producer of X to be able to hire labour and capital and to purchase materials at fixed rates, and to apply these to land.

First let him cultivate only one plot and vary his production (x_1) by varying the amounts of labour (y_1) and material (y_2).

His production is $x_1 = F(y_1 y_2)$ and, if p is the selling price which he cannot affect, he maximizes $px_1 - p'x_1$, where p' is his cost of production per unit.

The necessary equations are

$$p'x = \pi_1 y_1 + \pi_2 y_2,$$

$$\frac{1}{\pi_1} F_{y_1} = \frac{1}{\pi_2} F_{y_2},$$

$$x = F(y_1 y_2),$$

resulting after eliminating y_1 and y_2 in $p' = \phi_1(x)$ say.

Under conditions of decreasing return $\phi'_1(x)$ is positive.

x_1 is then given by

$$p = D_{x_1}(p'x_1) = \phi_1(x_1) + x_1 \phi'_1(x_1) = p'_m.$$

His maximum profit is

$$(p'_m - p')x_1 = x_1^2 \cdot \phi'_1(x_1).$$

Similarly he cultivates all plots for which

$$p = \phi_1(x) + x_1 \phi'_1(x)$$

gives a positive root.

His local margin of cultivation is where the root of this equation is zero.

The intensive margin on each cultivated plot is when $p = p'_m$, where $p'_m \delta x$ is expense of increasing the product from x to $x + \delta x$.

The profit $x_1^2\phi'_1(x_1)$ is the rent which can be exacted for plot 1, if his labour and interest on capital are included in y_1 and y_2. If he can command elsewhere a price P, for his ability (in excess of his labour wage) he would pay rent

$$\sum x_1^2 \phi'_1(x_1) - P,$$

the summation being extended over all the plots.

The above analysis applies with verbal changes to rent of urban land.

§ 3. Taxation in the case of competition.

Let a tax τ per unit X_r be imposed, to be paid by the producer.

Isolate demand $f(x)$ and supply $\phi(x)$ of X_r, ignoring other commodities.

Write $\psi(x) = f(x) - \phi(x)$.

Before tax, let equilibrium be at $\psi(x_1) = 0$.

After tax, ,,   ,,   ,, $\psi(x_1 - \xi) = \tau$.

$$\therefore \tau = -\xi\psi'(x_1) + \tfrac{1}{2}\xi^2\psi''(x_1) - \dots.*$$

Receipt from tax $R = \tau(x_1 - \xi)$,

$$\therefore R = -x_1\xi\psi'(x_1) + \xi^2\psi'(x_1) + \tfrac{1}{2}\xi^2 x_1\psi''(x_1) + \text{terms in } \xi^3, \&c.$$

Consumers' loss of utility expressed in money is

$$C = \int_0^{x_1} f(x)\,dx - x_1 f(x_1) - \int_0^{x_1-\xi} f(x)\,dx + (x_1 - \xi)f(x_1 - \xi)$$

$$= \int_{x_1-\xi}^{x_1} f(x)\,dx - x_1 f(x_1) + (x_1 - \xi)f(x_1 - \xi).$$

Write $x = x' + x_1 - \xi$.

$$C = \int_0^{\xi} f(x_1 - \xi + x')\,dx' - x_1 f(x_1) + (x_1 - \xi)f(x_1 - \xi)$$

$$= \int_0^{\xi} \left\{ f(x_1 - \xi) + x'f'(x_1 - \xi) + \frac{x'^2}{2}f''(x_1 - \xi) + \dots \right\}dx' - x_1 f(x_1)$$
$$+ (x_1 - \xi)f(x_1 - \xi)$$

$$= \xi f(x_1 - \xi) + \tfrac{1}{2}\xi^2 f'(x_1 - \xi) + \tfrac{1}{6}\xi^3 f''(x_1 - \xi) + \dots - x_1 f(x_1)$$
$$- \xi f'(x_1 - \xi) + x_1\left\{ f(x_1) - \xi f'(x_1) + \tfrac{1}{2}\xi^2 f''(x_1) - \dots \right\}$$

$$= -x_1\xi f'(x_1) + \tfrac{1}{2}\xi^2\left\{ f'(x_1) + x_1 f''(x_1) \right\} + \text{terms in } \xi^3.$$

* See Appendix, p. 84.

Let Q be the position of equilibrium before taxation, L after.

$ON = x_1 \quad NQ = f(x_1) = \phi(x_1) \quad MN = \xi$

QN, LM are perpendicular, and KT, QH, LS parallel, to OX

$\tau = KL = JQ\left(-f'(x_1) + \phi'(x_1)\right)$ approx. $= -\xi \cdot \psi'(x_1)$

$C = \text{area } QHSL = \tfrac{1}{2}JL(HQ+SL) = \tfrac{1}{2}\xi\left(-f'(x_1)\right)(2x_1-\xi)$
$\qquad\qquad\qquad\qquad\qquad\qquad\qquad\qquad$ approx.

$R = \text{area } KTSL = KL \cdot KT = \tau(x_1-\xi)$

Let $P = \text{area } QHTK = \tfrac{1}{2}KL(HQ+SL) = \tfrac{1}{2}\xi\phi'(x_1)(2x_1-\xi)$
$\qquad\qquad\qquad\qquad\qquad\qquad\qquad\qquad$ approx.

$C+P-R = \text{area } KLQ = \tfrac{1}{2}KL \cdot JQ = \tfrac{1}{2}\tau\xi$ approx.

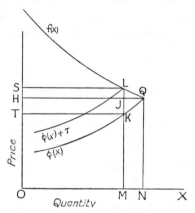

Competition : Decreasing Return.

FIGURE 19.

The approximation assumes that the curvature of the arcs LQ and KQ is negligible.

Similar diagrams can be drawn to illustrate other cases.

Competition being assumed, in increasing return where producer makes no profit

$C-R = x_1\xi\left(-\phi'(x_1)\right) + \xi^2\left\{-\tfrac{1}{2}f'(x_1)+\phi'(x_1)\right\} + \tfrac{1}{2}\xi^2 x_1\phi''(x_1).$

In constant return

$$C-R = \tfrac{1}{2}\xi^2\left\{-f'(x_1)\right\}.$$

In both cases terms involving ξ^3 are neglected.

With decreasing return, where the supply curve is that

aggregated from those of the separate producers, the producer's aggregate loss of profit is

$$P = x_1 \cdot \phi(x_1) - \int_0^{x_1} \phi(x) \cdot dx - (x_1 - \xi) \cdot \phi(x_1 - \xi) + \int_0^{x_1 - \xi} \phi(x) \cdot dx$$

$$= \text{(after reduction as in the case of } C\text{)}$$
$$x_1 \xi \phi'(x_1) - \tfrac{1}{2}\xi^2 \{\phi'(x_1) + x_1 \phi''(x_1)\} + \text{terms in } \xi^3.$$

$$\therefore C + P - R = \tfrac{1}{2}\xi^2(\phi'(x_1) - f'(x_1)), \text{ if } \xi^3 \text{ is neglected.}$$

Hence in all cases the public, producer and consumer together, lose more than the revenue gains. In the case of increasing return the loss is greater than in that of decreasing return.

Now, if we neglect $f''(x)$ and $\phi''(x)$ and regard the part of the supply and demand curves involved as straight lines, we have

$$\frac{C}{P} = \frac{-f'(x_1)}{\phi'(x_1)} = \frac{-e}{\eta},$$

if e and η are the elasticities of supply and demand at x_1.

The increase of price is

$$f(x_1 - \xi) - f(x_1) = -\xi \cdot f'(x_1),$$

now $f''(x)$ is taken as 0,

$$= \tau \cdot \frac{-f'(x_1)}{-f'(x_1) + \phi'(x_1)} = \frac{e}{e - \eta} \cdot \tau.$$

In constant return the increase of price is τ, in increasing return it is greater, and in decreasing return, less than τ.

Tax receipts are at a *maximum* when τ is so chosen that if x_τ is the amount exchanged, $x_\tau \cdot \psi(x_\tau)$ is a maximum. [This is where a monopolist untaxed would fix the quantity produced.]

If $f'(x)$ and $\phi'(x)$ are taken as constant, which is a less reasonable assumption than before, since the change of x is now considerable, and x_1 is the amount that would have been exchanged if there had been no tax, it is easily shown that (p. 59)

$$x_\tau = \tfrac{1}{2}x_1, \text{ and therefore } \xi = x_\tau, \quad \tau = -\tfrac{1}{2}x_1 \cdot \psi'(x_1),$$

$$R = -\tfrac{1}{4}x_1^2 \psi'(x_1), \quad C = \tfrac{3}{8}x_1^2 (-f_1'(x_1)), \quad P = \tfrac{3}{8}x_1^2 \cdot \phi'(x_1),$$

$$C + P - R = \tfrac{1}{2}R \text{ in decreasing return,}$$

$$C - R = \tfrac{1}{2}R \text{ in constant return.}$$

The excess of the loss to the public over the gain to the revenue is half the revenue receipts in these cases.

In increasing return

$$C - R = \tfrac{1}{8}x_1^2\left(-f'(x_1) - 2\phi'(x_1)\right)$$
$$= \tfrac{1}{2}R + \tfrac{3}{8}x_1^2\left(-\phi'(x_1)\right),$$

and the excess of the loss is even greater.

§ 4. Taxation in the case of producer's monopoly.

At tax τ, a monopolist maximizes $(\psi(x) - \tau)x$, say at x_τ, where

$$\psi(x_\tau) + x_\tau\psi'(x_\tau) = \tau,$$
$$R = \tau x_\tau = x_\tau\{\psi(x_\tau) + x_\tau\psi'(x_\tau)\}.$$

Without tax x_1 would have been produced, where

$$\psi(x_1) + x_1\psi'(x_1) = 0.$$

Then P, now taken as loss of profit and tax,

$$= x_1\psi(x_1) - x_\tau(\psi(x_\tau) - \tau),$$

and

$$C = \int_{x_\tau}^{x_1}f(x)\,dx - x_1f(x_1) + x_\tau f(x_\tau).$$

$$C + P - R = -x_1\phi(x_1) + x_\tau\phi(x_\tau) + \int_{x_\tau}^{x_1}f(x)\,dx.$$

Write $x_1 = x_\tau + \xi$ and take the case where the supply and demand are straight lines, so that

$$f''(x) = \phi''(x_1) = \psi''(x_1) = 0.$$

Then, expanding by Taylor's series,* we find

$$\tau = \psi(x_1 - \xi) + (x_1 - \xi)\psi'(x_1 - \xi) = -2\xi\psi'(x_1),$$
$$R = -2x_\tau\xi\psi'(x_1), \quad C = -\tfrac{1}{2}f'(x_1)\cdot\xi(2x_1 - \xi),$$
$$P = x_1\psi(x_1) - (x_1 - \xi)(\psi(x_1) - \xi\psi'(x_1)) + R$$
$$= \xi\psi(x_1) - (x_1 - \xi)\frac{\xi}{x}\psi(x_1) + R = \frac{\xi^2}{x_1}\psi(x_1) + R$$
$$= -\xi^2\psi'(x_1) + R = \psi'(x_1)\cdot(\xi^2 - 2x_1\xi),$$
$$C + P - R = \xi^2\phi'(x_1) - (\tfrac{1}{2}\xi^2 + \xi x_1)f'(x_1).$$

* See Appendix, p. 84.

Hence on the same assumption

$$\frac{C}{P} = \frac{f'(x_1)}{2\,\psi'(x_1)} = \frac{e}{2\,(e-\eta)}.$$

Hence $C = \frac{1}{2}P$ in constant return,

$\qquad\qquad C > \frac{1}{2}P$ in increasing return, and $C = P$, if for example
$$\phi' = \frac{1}{2}f',$$

and $\qquad C < \frac{1}{2}P$ in decreasing return.

In constant return,

$$C + P - R = \xi\,(x_1 + \tfrac{1}{2}\xi)\,(-f'(x_1)) = \frac{\tau}{2}(x_1 + \tfrac{1}{2}\xi).$$

In decreasing return, add $\xi^2\,\phi'(x_1)$ to this expression.
In increasing return, if for example $\phi'(x) = \frac{1}{2}f'(x)$,

$$C + P - R = x_1\xi\,(-f'(x_1)) = x_1\tau.$$

In the same case of monopoly, R is a maximum when the quantity sold after the tax is imposed makes $x\,(\psi(x) + x\psi'(x))$ a maximum, and then

$$\psi(x_\tau) + 3\,x_\tau\,\psi'(x_\tau) + x^2_\tau\,\psi''(x_\tau) = 0.$$

Take again the case where

$$f''(x) = \phi''(x) = \psi''(x) = 0.$$

Before the tax was imposed

$$\psi(x_1) + x_1\,\psi'(x_1) = 0.$$

Then, if $x_1 = x_\tau + \xi$,

$$0 = \psi(x_1 - \xi) + 3\,(x_1 - \xi)\,\psi'(x) = -\xi\psi'(x_1) + (2\,x_1 - 3\xi)\cdot\psi'(x_1)\cdot$$

$$\therefore\ \xi = \tfrac{1}{2}x_1 \text{ and } x_\tau = \tfrac{1}{2}x_1.$$

$$\tau = -2\,\xi\psi'(x_1), \text{ as before, } = -x_1\psi'(x_1) = \psi(x_1).$$

Hence the maximum yield is when the rate of tax equals the difference between the monopolist's selling and cost prices before the tax.

$R = $ yield of tax $= \frac{1}{2}x_1\psi(x_1)$.

$P = -\xi^2\psi'(x_1) + R = \frac{3}{4}x\ \psi(x_1) = \frac{3}{2}R$.

$C = -\frac{3}{8}x_1{}^2f'(x_1),\ = \frac{3}{4}R$ in constant return.

$C + P - R = \frac{1}{2}R + \frac{3}{8}x_1{}^2\,(-f'(x_1)) = \frac{5}{4}R$ in constant return.

In increasing return in the case when $\phi' = \frac{1}{2}f'$, $C = P = \frac{3}{2}R$, and $C + P - R = 2R$.

Under monopoly, the increase of price (whether R is maximized or not) is

$$f(x - \xi) - f(x_1) = -\xi f'(x_1) + \frac{\xi^2}{2}f''(x_1) - + \ldots,$$

$$= \frac{\tau}{2} \cdot \frac{f'(x_1)}{\psi'(x_1)} = \frac{\tau}{2} \cdot \frac{e}{e - \eta}, \text{ if } f''(x_1) \text{ is 0 or if } \xi^2 \text{ is negligible.}$$

We have then from the equation for C given above

$$C = \left(x_1 - \frac{\xi}{2}\right) \times \text{increase of price,}$$

$$= \frac{x_1 + x_\tau}{2} \times \text{increase of price.}$$

In constant return, increase of price is $\dfrac{\tau}{2}$.

In decreasing   „   „   „   „ $< \dfrac{\tau}{2}$

In increasing   „   „   „   „ $> \dfrac{\tau}{2}$, and, in the case where $\phi' = \frac{1}{2}f'$, $= \tau$.

Under monopoly, if the tax is not per unit but a lump sum, the price is unaffected and the amount sold unaffected; the whole is paid by monopolist and can theoretically be increased till it nullifies his profit, and $R = x_1\psi(x_1)$, viz. twice the maximum under a tax per unit.

NOTE.—The term ' consumer's surplus', applied to $U(x) - xf(x)$, has given rise to misconception, and has been avoided here. But it is useful to distinguish two parts of C (pp. 72-3), viz. $U(x_1) - U(x_1 - \xi)$, or $MLQN$ (figure 19), which is the loss of utility, and $(x_1 - \xi)f(x_1 - \xi) - x_1 f(x_1)$, or $OSLM - OHQN$, which is the increase of cost (which is negative for large elasticity). The two together give $QHSL$ or C.

Thus if weekly purchases of tobacco before and after taxation were 4 oz. at 3d. and 3 oz. at 5d., one ounce worth approximately 4d. is lost and 3d. more is spent. The loss to the consumer in this case is taken as 7d.

APPENDIX

SUMMARY OF THE MATHEMATICAL IDEAS AND FORMULAE USED

THE following notes are only likely to be useful to those who have at some time studied the elements of the calculus in an ordinary course. Only a very limited region of the calculus is used in ordinary economic reasoning, but in some respects it is of a kind to which prominence is not given in the usual mathematical training, while much attention is devoted to other aspects of its use, in physics, &c. It has therefore seemed worth while to trace the theory of the calculus from the beginning up to the theorems and methods used in the text, to enable readers to refresh their memories about the particular results wanted and to become used to the notation adopted. The definitions and proofs are not rigid in the mathematical sense, and any careful reader will detect numerous lacunae.

The results may, however, be accepted as true in the sense and with the limitations used in the text, and complete proofs can readily be found by those who have sensitive mathematical consciences.

Functions.

If two variables x and y are so related that y is determinate when x is given, y is said to be an (explicit) function of x. This relationship is written $y = f(x)$; but since several functions may be involved in the same problem, variants of f (e.g. F, ϕ...) or other letters (χ, U...) are used also to express the functions.

If two or more variables x, y, z...determine another variable, u, then $u = f(x, y, z...)$.

If x and y are connected by any equation such as

$$x + y + 8 = 0, \quad x^2 + 2y^2 - 7 = 0, \quad \sin(x+y) - 3 = 0,$$

the relationship may be written generally as

$$f(x, y) = 0.$$

f is then said to be an *implicit* function.

It is often not necessary to know the form of the function nor to be able to evaluate it. Important relations can be established and results obtained from the mere knowledge that certain quantities determine others.

The function contains numbers and often constants (generally written a, b, c...), that is quantities which remain unchanged while x, y... vary. It is necessary to know these numbers and constants if the function is to be evaluated numerically.

$f(x_1)$ means the value of $f(x)$ when the particular value x_1 is given to the general variable x.

$f(x)$ is said to be continuous over the range $x = a$ to $x = b$, when x can take all values from a to b, to each of which there is a real finite value of $f(x)$, and when, if x makes a finite change, the change in $f(x)$ is also finite. This may be explained by saying that a continuous function can be graphically represented by a line drawn without the pen leaving the paper or marking a sharp angle. The definition here given is only a preliminary or popular one, but it is sufficient for the sequel.

Derived functions or differential coefficients.

Let the values of y corresponding to a range of values of x be plotted on squared paper, so that when $x = OM$, $y = MP$, and as x increases from OM to ON, P moves along a curve (or straight line) to Q. The line PQ is the *graph* of the function; $y = f(x)$ is the *equation* of the curve (Figure A, p. 81).

The point P is written (x, y). x and y are the *co-ordinates* of P; x is the *abscissa*; y the *ordinate*; OX, OY are the *axes of reference*.

Let the co-ordinates of Q be $x + h$ and $y + k$, so that (if PL is parallel to OX and meets NQ in L) $MN = h$, $LQ = k$.

Draw PT to touch the curve at P, and join PQ and produce it. Then

$$\tan QPL = LQ \div PL = k/h = (y + k - y)/h = (f(x + h) - f(x))/h.$$

Now let Q approach P along the curve. The chord PQ rotates about P, till as Q reaches P it coincides with PT, and the angle QPL becomes the angle $TPL = \theta$, say.

Tan θ is the limit of $(f(x+h)-f(x))/h$, when h approaches, and finally becomes, zero. This result is written

$$\tan \theta = \underset{}{\mathrm{L}^t} \frac{f(x+h)-f(x)}{h} \; (h \to 0) = D_x y* = f'(x),$$

each of these expressions being a convenient way of writing the process and result briefly.

For example, the graph in Figure **A** represents

$$y = f(x) = 1 + 7x - x^2.$$

$$\text{Tan } \theta = D_x y = f'(x)$$
$$= \underset{}{\mathrm{L}^t} \frac{\{1 + 7(x+h) - (x+h)^2\} - \{1 + 7x - x^2\}}{h} \; (h \to 0)$$
$$= \underset{}{\mathrm{L}^t} \frac{7h - 2hx - h^2}{h} = 7 - 2x.$$

Thus when $x = 2$ (and $y = 11$), the point P in the figure,

$$f'(x) = 7 - 4 = 3.$$

The tangent at P rises 3 units vertically to 1 unit horizontally. The *gradient* is 3.

$f'(x)$ is the rate of increase of $f(x)$ per unit change of x at the point x.

$f'(x)$ is called the *derived function*, the *derivative*, the *differential coefficient* or the *gradient* of $f(x)$.

When $f'(x)$ is positive the curve rises to the right. Where $f'(x)$ is zero ($x = 3\frac{1}{2}$ in the figure) the curve ceases to rise. When $f'(x)$ is negative ($x > 3\frac{1}{2}$) the curve falls.

The *maximum* of $f(x)$ is when $f'(x) = 0$, if (as in this case) $f'(x)$ changes from positive to negative as x increases through the maximal position, that is if at this point the curve is concave to OX (and above it).

If now we take the curve

$$y = x^2 - 7x + 15, \; f'(x) = 2x - 7. \quad \text{(Figure B.)}$$
$$f'(x) = 0, \text{ when } x = 3\frac{1}{2}.$$
$$f'(x) < 0, \text{ when } x < 3\frac{1}{2}. \quad f'(x) > 0, \text{ when } x > 3\frac{1}{2}.$$
$$f(x) \text{ is a minimum when } x = 3\frac{1}{2}.$$

---

* Formerly this expression was written $\frac{dy}{dx}$. Since this suggests a fraction and not the result of a process, the form here used is to be preferred.

The *minimum* of $f(x)$ is when $f'(x) = 0$ and the curve is convex to OX (and above it).

These results are general. The first test for the presence of a maximum or minimum is that $f'(x) = 0$. To decide whether this gives a maximum or gives a minimum it is necessary to

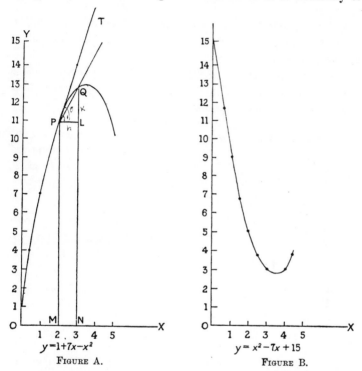

$$y = 1 + 7x - x^2$$

FIGURE A.

$$y = x^2 - 7x + 15$$

FIGURE B.

know the *sign* of $f'(x)$ for values of x to the left and right of the maximal position, unless (as is very often the case) we know *a priori* which to expect.

Successive differentiation. Expansions.

The process of differentiation can of course be applied to the derived function. We thus obtain the *second derivative*, and so on successively.

Thus in the first example taken,

$$f'(x) = 7 - 2x.$$

The second derivative

$$D^2{}_x y = f''(x) = \underset{}{\text{L}}^t \frac{7 - 2(x+h) - (7 - 2x)}{h}\ (h \to 0) = -2.$$

If $f''(x)$ is negative, $f'(x)$ if positive is becoming less as x increases, and if negative is becoming numerically greater negatively.

A little consideration will show that if $f''(x)$ is negative the curve is concave to OX (if above it), and if $f''(x)$ is positive the curve is convex.

The complete test for a maximum (if $f''(x)$ is not zero) is that $f'(x) = 0$ and $f''(x)$ is negative, and for a minimum that $f'(x) = 0$ and $f''(x)$ is positive.

In the adjacent Figure (C) of a convex curve, PT is the tangent at P and meets the ordinate of a neighbouring point Q at T. PL is parallel to OX.

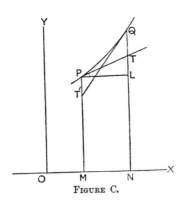

FIGURE C.

Write

$$\delta x = h = MN, \quad \delta y = k = LQ.$$

δx and δy are small finite increments or 'infinitesimals' of x and y.

$$LT = PL \tan LPT = hf'(x).$$
$$\delta y = NQ - MP$$
$$= f(x+h) - f(x) = LQ$$
$$= LT + TQ = f'(x) . \delta x + TQ.$$

TQ, the departure of the curve from its tangent, diminishes as Q approaches P.

We shall immediately give an informal proof that TQ is comparable with h^2, i.e. with $(\delta x)^2$. Assuming this we have

$$\delta y = f'(x) . \delta x + \text{a quantity involving } (\delta x)^2 \quad . \quad . \quad \text{Formula 1.}$$

$$\therefore \frac{\delta y}{\delta x} = f'(x) + \text{a quantity involving } \delta x, \text{ and in the limit,}$$

when h is zero, $\dfrac{\delta y}{\delta x} = D_x y$.

To obtain a rough proof of the proposition just used, draw the tangent at Q to meet MP at T'. The gradient of this tangent is $f'(x+h)$. In the case where Q is above T, it is evident (the curve being continuous and h small) that QT' cuts PL between P and L and therefore $QL < hf'(x+h)$. Hence

$$hf'(x) < f(x+h) - f(x) < hf'(x+h),$$

and $\qquad f(x+h) - f(x) = hf'(x+ch),$

where $x+ch$ is some value intermediate between x and $x+h$, and continuity is assumed.

The same result is obtained if the curve is concave, and this proposition is true for all continuous functions.

Hence similarly

$$f'(x+ch) - f'(x) = chf''(x+c_1 h)$$

where c_1, is intermediate between 1 and c.

Combining these results, we have

$$\delta y = f(x+h) - f(x) = hf'(x) + ch^2 f''(x+c_1 h),$$

where c and c_1 are proper fractions, and $h = \delta x$.

A change in y is therefore obtained approximately by multiplying the change in x by the first derived function, the equation being the more exact the smaller the change in x.

This result is fundamental in a considerable part of the application to Economics.

A rough examination of the general expansion of $f(x+h)$ can be obtained as follows.

Take x as fixed, say x_0, and h as variable. Write

$$f(x_0 + h) = F(h).$$

Thus in Figure C let

$$OM = x_0, \quad MP = f(x_0), \quad NQ = f(x_0 + h) = F(h).$$

Suppose that $F(h)$ is expansible in ascending powers of h with all the terms finite and the series convergent, i. e. tends to a unique finite limit when the number of terms is increased indefinitely.

Write $F(h) = a_0 + a_1 h + a_2 h^2 + a_3 h^3 + a_4 h^4 + \dots$, where $a_0, a_1 \dots$ are constants to be determined.

Differentiate successively with regard to h.

$$F'(h) = a_1 + 2a_2 h + 3a_3 h^2 + 4a_4 h^3 + \dots$$
$$F''(h) = 2a_2 + 3 \cdot 2a_3 h + 4 \cdot 3a_4 h^2 + \dots$$
$$F'''(h) = 3 \cdot 2a_3 + 4 \cdot 3 \cdot 2a_4 h + \dots.$$

In each of these equations take the case where $h = 0$.

$$a_0 = F(0), \quad a_1 = F'(0), \quad a_2 = \frac{1}{2} F''(0),$$

$$a_3 = \frac{1}{2 \cdot 3} F'''(0), \quad \ldots a_r = \frac{1}{r!} F^r(0) \ldots,$$

where $F'(0)$ is the result of writing $h = 0$ after $F(h)$ is differentiated and so on.

Then $F'(0)$ is the gradient of the curve PQ at P and therefore is the same as $f'(x_0)$, that is the result of writing $x = x_0$ in the derivative of $f(x)$. Similarly $F''(0) = f''(x_0)$ and so on.

We have then

$$f(x_0 + h) = F(h) = f(x_0) + hf'(x_0)$$
$$+ \frac{1}{2} h^2 f''(x_0) + \ldots \frac{1}{r!} h^r f^r(x_0) + \ldots \qquad \text{Formula 2,}$$

the process being continued as far as we please.

This is Taylor's Series.

In the functions used in the text it is generally the case that the successive terms become rapidly smaller over the part of the curves that are considered in the neighbourhood of equilibrium. Such an assumption is much more hazardous when larger changes are considered, as in the cases of taxation and monopoly (pp. 60 and 75 seq).

Standard derivatives and rules of differentiation.

The following are standard derived functions, as shown in any text-book on the calculus :

$$D_x(x^n) = nx^{n-1},$$

where n is any positive or negative integer or fraction ;

e.g. $$D_x \sqrt{x} = \frac{1}{2} x^{-\frac{1}{2}}.$$

$$D_x(a^x) = a^x \cdot \log_e a. \quad D_x(e^x) = e^x.$$

$$D_x(\log_a x) = \frac{1}{x} \cdot \log_a e. \quad D_x(\log_e x) = \frac{1}{x}.$$

$$D_x(\sin x) = \cos x, \quad D_x(\cos x) = -\sin x, \quad D_x(\tan x) = \sec^2 x,$$

where x is the radian measure of the angle.

Also the following working rules are easily proved from the definition of a derived function :

$$D_x\left(af(x)\right) = a \cdot f'(x) ;$$

e.g. $D_x(3x) = 3, \ D_x(3x^2) = 3 \times 2x = 6x.$

$$D_x f(ax) = af'(ax) ;$$

e.g. $D_x \sin(ax) = a \cos ax.$

$$D_x\left(f(x) + a\right) = f'(x) ;$$

e.g. $D_x(x^2 + 3) = 2x.$

$$D_x f(x + a) = f'(x + a) ;$$

e.g. $D_x(x + a)^2 = 2(x + a),$ for if $f(x) = x^2, f'(x) = 2x.$

These rules may be combined, thus :

$$D_x\left\{af(bx + c) + d\right\} = ab \cdot f'(bx + c) ;$$

e.g. $D_x\{2 \sin(3x + 4) + 5\} = 2 \times 3 \cos(3x + 4) = 6 \cos(3x + 4).$

If $f(x)$ and $\phi(x)$ are two functions of x, the following rules can be obtained :

$$D_x\left\{f(x) \pm \phi(x)\right\} = f'(x) \pm \phi'(x) ;$$

e.g. $D_x(x^2 + \log_e x) = 2x + 1/x.$

$$D_x\left\{f(x) \times \phi(x)\right\} = f'(x) \times \phi(x) + f(x) \times \phi'(x) ;$$

e.g. $D_x(x^2 \sin x) = 2x \sin x + x^2 \cos x.$

$$D_x\left\{f(x) \div \phi(x)\right\} = \left\{f'(x) \times \phi(x) - f(x) \times \phi'(x)\right\} \div (\phi(x))^2 ;$$

e.g. $D_x(\tan x) = D_x(\sin x \div \cos x)$
$$= \{\cos x \times \cos x - \sin x \times (-\sin x)\} \div \cos^2 x$$
$$= (\cos^2 x + \sin^2 x) \div \cos^2 x = 1 + \tan^2 x = \sec^2 x,$$

as above.

If $y = F(u)$, where $u = f(x)$,

$$\frac{\delta y}{\delta x} = \frac{\delta y}{\delta u} \times \frac{\delta u}{\delta x} = \frac{F(u + \delta u) - F(u)}{\delta u} \times \frac{f(x + \delta x) - f(x)}{\delta x},$$

identically.

In the limit, obtained by diminishing δx and consequently δu and δy also,

$$D_x y = D_u F(u) \times D_x f(x) ;$$

e.g. if F stands for $\log_e$, f for sin, and so $u = \sin x$,

$$D_x \{\log_e (\sin x)\} = D_u (\log_e u) \times D_x (\sin x)$$
$$= \frac{1}{u} \times \cos x = \frac{1}{\sin x} \times \cos x = \cot x.$$
$$D_x \{\sin (x^2)\} = 2x \cos (x^2).$$

These forms and rules are sufficient for the differentiation of common functions of one variable.

Functions of two or more variables. Partial differentiation.

Let a variable z depend on two other variables x and y, so that $z = f(x, y)$, and let x and y depend on another variable t. Required to connect a change in t with a change in z.

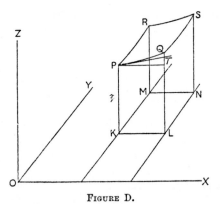

FIGURE D.

To fix ideas, suppose a point to be moving in the plane XOY (Figure D), and at any time t to be at the point $K(x, y)$. Let a vertical $KP(z)$ be erected whose height is $f(x, y)$. Then as the point moves about the plane XOY, P will move always vertically over the point on a surface whose equation is

$$z = f(x, y).$$

Consider movements parallel to OX, i.e. to the plane ZOX.

If the point moves from K to L, y is constant (say y_1) while x varies, and P traces out a plane curve PQ. The gradient at

P of this curve is $D_x f(x, y_1)$, that is the result of differentiating $f(x, y_1)$ where y_1 does not vary. This expression is variously written

$$D_x(z) \ (y \ \text{const}), \ \frac{\partial z}{\partial x}, \ f'(x, y) \ (y \ \text{const}), \ f_x, \ \text{and} \ z_x \quad \text{Formula 3.}$$

f_x is at once the briefest and most convenient of these forms. It means the result of the process of differentiation with respect to x applied to the function, y being kept constant; e.g. if

$$f(x, y) = ax^2 + by^2, \ f_x = 2ax, \ f_y = 2by.$$

This quantity f_x is called the *partial derived function* (or derivative or differential coefficient) with respect to x.

If the point P had moved along the tangent at P in the plane of PQ it would have risen hf_x, to T, when x increased to $x + h$, h being KL.

Similarly if we take movements parallel to OY or the plane ZOY, let the point in the plane XOY move from K to M ($KM = k$) and P trace the curve PR. Its initial gradient would be f_y, and if it had moved along the tangent to PR it would have risen kf_y.

Now if h and k are small the heights of Q and R only differ from those obtained at T and the corresponding point under R by quantities involving h^2 and k^2 (by formula 1), which are therefore very small. The rises in the two paths are therefore very nearly hf_x and kf_y.

Further it can be shown (though the complete proof is difficult) that the rise along the path QS, where $KLNM$ is a rectangle and NS is vertical, differs from the rise along PR only by a quantity of the order hk.

If, then, the point in the plane XOY moves from K to N by any path and in consequence a line PS is traced on the surface, the increase of height from P to S differs from $hf_x + kf_y$ by a quantity involving h^2, k^2, or hk as factors. Write δz for this increase.

$$\delta z = z + \delta z - z = f(x + h, y + k) - f(x, y) = hf_x + kf_y$$
$$= f_x \cdot \delta x + f_y \cdot \delta y, \ \text{approximately}, \quad \text{Formula 4,}$$

where δx, δy are the increments of x and y.

Let δt be the time interval between K and N.

$$\frac{\delta z}{\delta t} = f_x \cdot \frac{\delta x}{\delta t} + f_y \cdot \frac{\delta y}{\delta t} \text{ approximately.}$$

Now proceed to the limit when δt approaches zero, and consequently δx, δy, δz approach zero, and the quantities h^2, k^2, hk, &c. which are omitted in Formula 4 vanish. We have

$$D_t z = f_x \cdot D_t x + f_y \cdot D_t y.$$

Thus if $z = ax^2 + by^2$, where $x = \cos t$, $y = \sin t$, $f_x = 2ax$, $f_y = 2by$, $D_t x = -\sin t$, $D_t y = \cos t$, and

$$D_t z = -2ax \sin t + 2by \cos t$$
$$= -2a \cos t \sin t + 2b \sin t \cos t = (b-a) \sin 2t.$$

[This result may also be obtained directly by writing

$$z = a \cos^2 t + b \sin^2 t,$$

but it is not usual that the substitution should be so simple.]

The equation does not depend on the geometrical illustration but is universally true. For example we may take t, which is an independent variable completely at choice, as identical with x, and obtain
$$D_x z = f_x + f_y \cdot D_x y \quad . \quad . \quad . \quad \text{Formula 5.}$$

The result may be generalized to any number of variables, so that if $z = f(x_1 x_2 \ldots x_n)$,

$$D_t z = f_{x_1} \cdot D_t x_1 + f_{x_2} \cdot D_t x_2 + \ldots + f_{x_n} \cdot D_t x_n \ . \ \text{Formula 6,}$$

and $\quad D_{x_1} z = f_{x_1} + f_{x_2} \cdot D_{x_1} x_2 + \ldots + f_{x_n} \cdot D_{x_1} x_n \ . \ . \ \text{Formula 7.}$

e.g. If $\quad z = x_1{}^2 + x_2 x_3 + x_1 x_3 = f(x_1, x_2, x_3),$

$$f_{x_1} = 2x_1 + x_3, \quad f_{x_2} = x_3, \quad f_{x_3} = x_2 + x_1,$$

and $\quad D_{x_1} z = 2x_1 + x_3 + x_3 \cdot D_{x_1} x_2 + (x_2 + x_1) \cdot D_{x_1} x_3.$

We cannot evaluate this till we know the relationship between x_2 and x_1 and between x_3 and x_1.

The formula is commonly used as

$$\delta z = f_{x_1} \cdot \delta x_1 + f_{x_2}' \cdot \delta x_2 + \ldots + f_{x_n} \cdot \delta x_n \ . \ . \ \text{Formula 8,}$$

the variable on which $x_1, x_2 \ldots x_n$ depend not being named.

In this form it is very important in Economics.

In words, if a quantity z is dependent on variables $x_1, x_2 \dots x_n$, and these variables owing to a common cause have at the same time small increments $\delta x_1, \delta x_2 \dots$, whose squares and products are negligible, then the resulting increment in z is obtained by adding the increments in $x_1, x_2 \dots$, each multiplied by the partial derivative of z with respect to it computed on the assumption that the other x's do not vary.

Maxima and minima.

In Figure D (p. 86) z is a maximum or minimum where the tangent plane to the surface on which P moves is horizontal, so that when motion takes place in any direction the point starts along the plane and then falls below it (in the case of a maximum), or rises above it (in the case of a minimum). Where $z = f(x, y)$ and the tangent plane is horizontal, every line in it is horizontal, so that $f_x = 0 = f_y$, since these are the gradients in two of the directions.

More generally, when $z = f(x_1, x_2, \dots x_n)$, z cannot be a maximum or minimum, unless the effect of an infinitesimal change of any of the x's is to make $\delta z = 0$. From formula 8 this will be the case if

$$0 = f_{x_1} = f_{x_2} = \dots = f_{x_n} \quad . \quad . \quad . \quad \text{Formula 9.}$$

If we know *a priori*, as is often the case, that there is a maximum or a minimum in the region considered, these equations are sufficient. If not, terms of a higher degree in the increments must be examined.

[e.g. $z = x^2 + y^2 + 2x + 4y = (x+1)^2 + (y+2)^2 - 5$.

is clearly a minimum when $x = -1$, $y = -2$.

In this case, $f_x = 2x + 2$, $= 0$ if $x = -1$,

and $\qquad\qquad f_y = 2y + 4$, $= 0$ if $y = -2$.

If, however, $z = x^2 - 2xy + 2y^2 + 2x + 4y$,

$$f_x = 2x - 2y + 2, \quad f_y = -2x + 4y + 4,$$

and these are zero if $x = -4$, $y = -3$.

All we can say without further examination is that, if there is a maximum or minimum, it is at this point.]

It is often the case that $x_1, x_2 \ldots$ are not independent, but are connected with each other by one or more equations. The equations $0 = f_{x_1} = f_{x_2} = \ldots$ will not then in general be consistent with the connecting equations and the partial derivatives cannot all vanish together. The procedure then is to eliminate as many of the x's as there are connecting equations and proceed with the remainder taken as independent variables.

[Thus, if $z = x^2 + y^2 + 2x + 4y$ and $y = x + 2$,

$$z = x^2 + (x+2)^2 + 2x + 4(x+2) = 2x^2 + 10x + 12,$$

$$D_x z = 4x + 10, \ = 0 \ \text{if} \ x = -2 \cdot 5,$$

and, since $D^2_x z = 4$ and is positive, this gives a minimum for z, viz. $z = -\frac{1}{2}$.

This is the solution of the problem of finding the lowest point of the given surface in the vertical plane $y = x + 2$. The minimum of z without any restriction is -5 (p. 89) when $x = -1$, $y = -2$.]

The process of partial differentiation can be carried on successively. Thus, if $z = f(x, y)$, $f_{xx} = D_x(f_x)$, y const., is the second partial derived function of z with respect to x. It will measure the change of gradient of the curve PQ (Figure D, p. 86). Similarly f_{yy} measures the change of gradient of the curve PR. f_{xy} means $D_y(f_x)$, x const.; it can be shown, but not easily, that the same result is obtained from $D_x(f_y)$, y const., so that $f_{xy} = f_{yx}$. This measures the change in the gradient of the tangent parallel to the plane ZOX due to a movement of the section in the direction OY.

The more complete statement of the equation to which

$$\delta z = f_{x_1} \cdot \delta x_1 + f_{x_2} \cdot \delta x_2 + \ldots$$

is an approximation, is

$$\begin{aligned}
\delta z = &f_{x_1} \cdot \delta x_1 + f_{x_2} \cdot \delta x_2 + \ldots \\
&+ \tfrac{1}{2} \{ f_{x_1 x_1} (\delta x_1)^2 + f_{x_2 x_2} (\delta x_2)^2 + \ldots \\
&\qquad\qquad\qquad + 2 f_{x_1 x_2} \delta x_1 \cdot \delta x_2 + \ldots \} \\
&+ \text{terms involving cubes and higher powers of } \delta x,
\end{aligned}$$

Formula 10,

where all possible squares and products are included in { }.

An expansion by this formula is used on pp. 17–18 above.

An investigation of the complete formula can be made on the lines of that on pp. 83–4 and formula 2, as follows.

Write

$$f(x_0+h,\, y_0+k) = F(h,\, k)$$
$$= a + b_1 h + b_2 k + c_1 h^2 + c_2 hk + c_3 k^2 + d_1 h^3 + d_2 h^2 k$$
$$+ d_3 hk^2 + d_4 k^3 + \ldots.$$

Differentiate successively with respect to h and to k.

$$F_h = b_1 + 2c_1 h + c_2 k + 3d_1 h^2 + 2d_2 hk + d_3 k^2 + \ldots$$
$$F_{hh} = 2c_1 + 3 \cdot 2d_1 h + 2d_2 k + \ldots$$
$$F_{hk} = c_2 + 2d_2 h + 2d_3 k + \ldots.$$

Take the case in each equation where $h = 0 = k$.

$a = F(0,\, 0)$, $b_1 = F_h$, $c_1 = \frac{1}{2}F_{hh}$, $c_2 = F_{hk}$, and similarly $b_2 = F_k$, $c_3 = \frac{1}{2}F_{kk}$, in each case 0 being written for h and k after differentiation.

But then (as on p. 84) $F_h =$ the gradient at P of the curve PQ (Figure D, p. 86) $= f_{x_0}$, $F_k = f_{y_0}$, and similarly $F_{hh} = f_{x_0 x_0}$, &c.

$$\therefore \delta z = f(x_0+h,\, y_0+k) - f(x_0,\, y_0)$$
$$= hf_{x_0} + kf_{y_0} + \tfrac{1}{2}\left(h^2 f_{x_0 x_0} + 2hk f_{x_0 y_0} + k^2 f_{y_0 y_0}\right) \quad \text{Formula 11.}$$
$$+ \text{terms involving cubes of } h, \text{ &c.}$$

This result can easily be extended to any number of variables.

The above analysis is not a proof, but a determination of coefficients on the hypothesis that an expansion of this kind is possible.

With two variables $f(x, y)$ is a maximum or minimum at (x_0, y_0) only if $f_{x_0} = 0 = f_{y_0}$ and the complex term involving squares is of the same sign for all variations ; this is the case if $f_{x_0 x_0} \times f_{y_0 y_0} > (f_{x_0 y_0})^2$. Given this condition, $f(x_0, y_0)$ is a maximum or minimum according as $f_{x_0 x_0}$ is negative or positive.

Tangents.

It is often necessary to determine $D_x y$ when we are given $f(x, y) = 0$. $f(x, y) = 0$ is the equation of a plane curve and $D_x y$ is its gradient at any point (x, y).

Write $z = f(x, y)$.

Then $\delta z = f_x \cdot \delta x + f_y \cdot \delta y$ and $D_x z = f_x + f_y \cdot D_x y$ (pp. 87–8, formulae 4 and 5).

But since $z = f(x, y)$ is always zero, z is invariable, δz is zero, and $D_x z$ is zero.

$$\therefore \ 0 = f_x + f_y \cdot D_x y, \ \text{or} \ D_x y = -f_x/f_y.$$

The tangent at P, which we will call (x_1, y_1) (see Figure A, p. 81), is a line through (x_1, y_1) with gradient $D_x y$, and its equation is therefore

$$y - y_1 = (x - x_1) \tan TPL = (x - x_1) \cdot D_x y,$$

that is $\qquad (x - x_1) \cdot f_{x_1} + (y - y_1) \cdot f_{y_1} = 0 \ . \ .$ Formula 12,

where f_{x_1}, f_{y_1} are the results of writing $x = x_1$, $y = y_1$ in the partial derivatives of $f(x, y)$.

Thus, if $\qquad f(x, y) = ax^2 + 2hxy + ly^2 - c = 0,$

$$f_x = 2ax + 2hy, \ \ f_y = 2hx + 2by,$$

and the tangent at a point (x_1, y_1) on the curve is

$$(x - x_1)(2ax_1 + 2hy_1) + (y - y_1)(2hx_1 + 2by_1) = 0,$$

that is $\quad x(ax_1 + hy_1) + y(hx_1 + by_1) = ax_1{}^2 + 2hx_1 y_1 + by_1{}^2$
$$= c.$$

Notice that we can write an equation for $D_x y$ at once from such a curve as $ax^2 + 2hxy + by^2 - c = 0$, thus

$$2ax + 2hy + D_x y(2hx + 2by) = 0.$$

Integration.

Integration is the process of finding the original function when the derived function is given, and is the reverse of differentiation.

The symbol $\int$ signifies integration, and is defined by

$$\int f'(x) \cdot dx = f(x) + C,$$

where C (any constant) is introduced, since evidently

$$D_x \{ f(x) + C \} = f'(x).$$

Thus $\displaystyle \int x^{n-1} dx = \frac{1}{n} x^n + C$, since $D_x \left(\frac{1}{n} x^n \right) = x^{n-1}$.

The most important use of integration in the present connexion is in its relationship to areas.

Write $f'(x) = F(x)$.

Let CD be the graph of $y = F(x)$ from $x = a\,(OA)$ to $x = b\,(OB)$ (Figure E).

Divide AB into n equal parts

$$AN_1,\ N_1N_2\ldots \text{ each } = \delta x = (b-a)/n.$$

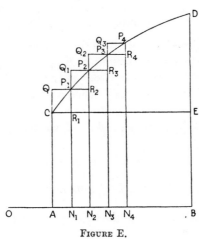

Let N_1P_1, $N_2P_2\ldots$ be ordinates, and complete the rectangles as in the figure.

Take the case of a curve that rises from C to D; other cases can readily be handled in the same way.

Let S, S' be the areas of the rectilinear figures

$$ACR_1P_1R_2P_2\ldots D, \text{ and } AQP_1Q_1P_2\ldots D.$$

Then the curvilinear area $ACP_1P_2\ldots D$ is intermediate between S and S'. $S' - S =$ sum of such areas as QR_1, $Q_1R_2\ldots$, and approximately $= \delta x \times ED$, where CE is parallel to AB. When n is large and therefore δx is small, this difference is negligible as compared with S, and S may be identified as the area of the curve.

Take n so large that $(\delta x)^2$ can be neglected.

Then from p. 82, formula 1,

$$f(a+\delta x)-f(a) = f'(a).\,\delta x = F(a).\,\delta x = AC.\,AN_1$$
$$f(a+2\delta x)-f(a+\delta x) = F(a+\delta x).\,\delta x = N_1P_1.\,N_1N_2$$

$$\cdot \quad \cdot \quad \cdot \quad \cdot \quad \cdot \quad \cdot \quad \cdot \quad \cdot \quad \cdot$$

$$f(a+n.\,\delta x)-f(a+\overline{n-1}\,\delta x) = F(a+\overline{n-1}\,\delta x).\,\delta x.$$

Adding we have, since $b = a + n\delta x$,

$$f(b)-f(a) = \text{sum of such areas as } ACR_1N, \; N_1P_1R_2N_2$$
$$= S \text{ with sufficient approximation}$$
$$= \text{area of curve.}$$

It is not difficult to verify that this final equation is absolutely true, when we suppose n indefinitely increased.

The area of the curve is the limit of the sum of the rectangles $F(x).\,\delta x$ from $x = a$ to $x = b$, when n is definitely increased,

$$= \text{limit of} \sum_a^b F(x).\,\delta x \text{ and this is written} \int_a^b F(x).\,dx.$$

The whole process is then summarized as

$$\text{area of curve} = \int_a^b F(x)\,dx = \int_a^b f'(x)\,dx = f(b)-f(a) \quad \text{Formula 13.}$$

Thus the area from OX to the curve $y = x^2$ is for any value of x

$$\int_0^x x^2\,dx = \tfrac{1}{3}x^3 - \tfrac{1}{3}.\,0 = \tfrac{1}{3}x^3.$$

Note on elimination.

Two linear equations

$$a_1x+b_1y+c_1 = 0, \quad c_2x+b_2y+c_2 = 0$$

give one pair of values of x and y, viz.

$$\frac{x}{b_1c_2-b_2c_1} = \frac{y}{c_1a_2-c_2a_1} = \frac{1}{a_1b_2-a_2b_1}.$$

Or we can eliminate y and obtain one equation for x,

$$(a_1b_2-a_2b_1)\,x + c_1b_2-c_2b_1 = 0.$$

From two equations involving three quantities x, y, z,

$$a_1x+b_1y+c_1z+d_1 = 0, \quad a_2x+b_2y+c_2z+d_2 = 0$$

we can eliminate one (z), and obtain a relation between the others,

$$(a_1 c_2 - a_2 c_1)\, x + (b_1 c_2 - b_2 c_1)\, y + d_1 c_2 - c_1 d_2 = 0.$$

Or we can say, from the first equation,

$$z = -\frac{1}{c_1}(a_1 x + b_1 y + d_1),$$

and when this value of z is written in the second equation we have

$$c_1(a_2 x + b_2 y + d_2) - c_2(a_1 x + b_1 y + d_1) = 0.$$

From this it can be seen that, if we have n linear equations connecting n quantities, we can determine the quantities separately, and that, if there are more than n quantities, we can eliminate $\overline{n-1}$ of them and obtain one equation involving the remainder; the procedure being virtually to solve for $\overline{n-1}$ selected quantities from $\overline{n-1}$ of the equations and substitute the results in the first equation.

With linear equations, if the quantities $a, b, c\ldots$ and n are given the solution is only a matter of patience. When we have the same problem involving squares, products, or other functions of $x, y\ldots$, the procedure is the same essentially, though it is not always possible to carry it out by simple methods.

Thus suppose we have three equations involving four quantities

$$f_1(u, v, x, y) = 0, \quad f_2(u, v, x, y) = 0, \quad f_3(u, v, x, y) = 0.$$

Solve the third as an equation in y, obtaining

$$y = F(u, v, x).$$

Put this value in the first and second, obtaining

$$F_1(u, v, x) = 0, \quad F_2(u, v, x) = 0.$$

Solve the last equation for x, obtaining $x = \phi(u, v)$ and put this value in $F_1(u, v, x) = 0$. We have then one equation involving u and v only, x and y being eliminated.

e.g. Eliminate x and y from the equations

$$u^2 + v^2 + x^2 = 20, \quad u^2 + 2v^2 + y^2 = 30, \quad u + x + y = 10.$$

From the second and third equations

$$u^2 + 2v^2 + (10 - u - x)^2 = 30$$
$$x = 10 - u \pm \sqrt{30 - u^2 - 2v^2}.$$

Then from the first

$$u^2 + v^2 + \left(10 - n \pm \sqrt{30 - u^2 - 2v^2}\right)^2 = 20,$$

which reduces to

$$5u^4 + v^4 + 6u^2v^2 - 120u^3 - 120uv^2$$
$$+ 900u^2 + 580v^2 - 2000u + 100 = 0.$$

Thus the actual solution rapidly becomes laborious in quite simple cases.

When there are as many (n) equations as variables, and $\overline{n-1}$ variables are eliminated, the remaining equation in one variable is not generally linear and there may be several real roots, each giving a set of simultaneous values for the variables. The equations are then said to have multiple solutions, and some further knowledge is necessary to know which is appropriate to the problem.

INDEX

A

Aggregate demand, 25.
Aggregate supply, 25.
Alternative demand, 38, 56, 66.
Alternative factors, 31.
Alternative supply, 66.
Alternative utility, 15, 17, 18, 56.

B

Barter, 5.
Bargaining locus, 8.
Bilateral monopoly, 62.

C

Capital, 42.
Commodities, 5.
Commodity equations, 21, 48, 50, 58.
Competition, 20; equilibrium in competition, 20, 58.
Complementary utility, 15, 16, 18, 56.
Composite demand, 65-6.
Composite supply, 65-6.
Constant return, 33, 36, 59, 69.
Consumers' combination, 62-5.
Consumers' goods, 65.
Consumers' surplus, 77.
Consumption, 6, 19.
Contract curve, 9, 10, 13.
Cost of production, 29, 31, 49.

D

Decreasing return, 34, 35, 37, 59, 63, 69, 73 seq.
Demand, 10; aggregate, 25; composite, 65, 66; derived, 68; elasticity of, 10; indirect, 65, 68; joint, 28, 65, 66, 67.
Demand curve, 10, 13; inclination of, 55.
Derivatives, 80; partial, 86, standard, 84-5.
Derived demand, 68.
Derived function, 79; second, 81; partial, 87.

D

Differential coefficient, 79.
Differentiation, 79; partial, 86; rules of, 84; successive, 81.
Diminishing return, v. decreasing.
Disutility, 40; marginal, 41, 43, 49.
Duopoly, 38.

E

Edgeworth, Prof. F. Y., 8.
Efficiency of money, 32.
Elasticity of demand, 10; of demand for factors, 44; of supply, 32.
Elimination, 94 seq.
Equations of demand, 50; for factors, 43; of equilibrium, 20-2, 51, 58; of supply, 43, 48.
Equilibrium, 8, 20, 51, 58, 59; stability of, 53.
Exchange, simple, 5; multiple, 19.
Expansions, 81.
Expenditure, 51.

F

Factors of production, 28; demand for, 43; share of, 44; supply of, 43, 48.
Functions, 78; derived, 79.

G

Goods, 1; consumers', 65; producers', 65.

I

Income, 51.
Increasing return, 33-6, 59, 63, 69, 73 seq.
Indifference curves, 6, 8, 10.
Indirect demand, 65, 68.
Independent utility, 15, 17, 18, 55.
Integral supply curve, 31.
Integration, 92.
Interdependence, 47, 52.